AGAINST NATURE
AND GOD

AGAINST NATURE AND GOD

The History of Women with
Clerical Ordination and the
Jurisdiction of Bishops

JOAN MORRIS

MOWBRAYS

LONDON AND OXFORD

© Joan Morris 1973

Printed and bound in Great Britain by
REDWOOD BURN LIMITED
Trowbridge & Esher

ISBN 0 264 66148 6

Library of Congress catalog card No: 72-89049

First published 1973 by the Macmillan Co., New York, N.Y.

First published in Great Britain 1974 by A. R. Mowbray & Co. Ltd

To *Barbara Ward*
who took so outstanding a part
in the Roman Synod 1971,
and to *Cardinal George B. Flahiff*
who so successfully broached
the subject of the role of women in
the Church at the same Synod.

ACKNOWLEDGMENTS

I wish to thank the many abbeys for the access given to their archives: the Abbey of Notre-Dame de Jouarre; Saint Croix of Poitiers; the Abbey of Las Huelgas de Burgos; the Cathedral Archives of Saint Waudru, Mons; the Bibliothèque Publique of Mons; the Collegiate of Covarrubias, Spain; the Municipal archives of Fontevrault, France; the Staat archives of Münster, Germany; the Cathedral archives of Conversano, Italy; the libraries of Bari, Lecce, and Brindisi. I am likewise thankful for the use of the large metropolitan libraries of East Berlin, of the Bibliothèque National of Paris, of the Vatican Library, and, last but not least, of the British Museum, on which I have relied very largely for a great deal of the information gathered in the present volume.

My thanks are also due to friends who have kindly assisted me by reading through the manuscript.

CONTENTS

INTRODUCTION

HISTORY MAY BE HIDDEN in many ways: it may be due to lack of care in the recording of events or to the loss of the records; to a language barrier or to the specialist's inability to see the forest for the trees. Unfortunately it may also be due to evasion of facts through prejudice. Worse, it may be due to a purposeful malicious hiding of events. Pliny the Elder tells us in his book *Natural History* that information was intentionally hidden regarding the work of women doctors, for according to the opinion of his day women should be quiet and as inconspicuous as possible so that after they were dead no one would know that they had lived. No wonder that evidence of the activities of women is not always easy to come by. Not only the ancients kept this conspiracy of silence through the centuries. The very stones bearing inscriptions cry out giving evidence of truths that have been carefully covered up. It is time for facts to be made known: women have contributed their fair share to the world's advancement.

In this book the hidden history of women who have held the jurisdiction of bishops is the subject of study. The Latin word for bishop, *episcopus,* is derived from the Greek word meaning "overseer." The women overseers, *episcopae*, of early Christian communities and the abbesses with quasi-episcopal jurisdiction show a tradition that lasted for centuries, and yet is little known, in which women had a prominent role. It is with a sense of urgency to reveal the truth that I relate the events of the most outstanding examples of women holding episcopal jurisdiction.

CHAPTER ONE

WOMEN OVERSEERS
OF CHURCHES

THE ROLE OF WOMEN in the Church of early Christian times has become hidden history. New Testament accounts show that women naturally assumed administrative duties in the apostolic period, for it is a noteworthy fact that all assemblies of Christian communities mentioned in the Acts of the Apostles and in the Epistles of Saint Paul are said to be in the houses of women: the church in the house of Chloe,[1] in the house of Lydia,[2] in the house of the mother of Mark,[3] in the house of Nympha,[4] in the house of Prisca (Priscilla) and Aquila.[5] Note that the name of Priscilla is put first.

As Christian assemblies were commonly held in the houses of women, why are commentators so surprised that Saint John in his second Epistle should address it to an "Elect Lady"; that is, to a woman who, obviously by the content of the letter, was in the position of overseer of a church community?

Prejudiced commentators, unwilling to consider the possibility of a woman holding a position of authority and overseer of an early Christian community, have tried to evade the issue by suggesting that the word *elect* might be the proper name of a woman —Electa. But since at the end of the epistle her sister is also called "elect," the suggestion was discarded as it was unlikely that two sisters with the same name would occur in one family.

A second explanation has been brought forward that is accepted by many today: the "Elect Lady" is considered to refer to a whole church in the same way as the term *mater ecclesia* is used to indicate the main church of the locality. But the word *Kyria* is nowhere else used in this sense, while we do know that the word *eklekta*—elect—was sometimes used to denote a clerically ordained person.[6] The "Elect Lady," addressed by Saint John, would therefore have been an elected person ordained to a special service of the Christian community, that is, as overseer. This does not mean that as an ordained overseer she also was ordained to consecrate the Holy Eucharist. We know that for reasons of the taboo of women during menstruation, they were considered unclean and liable to contaminate others and even to be under the domination of the devil.[7] Women were therefore withheld from the service of the altar, but they were able to undertake many other services such as overseers of communities that in apostolic times started in their homes.

The second Epistle of Saint John is very short, which is more characteristic of a private letter than of an epistle to be read in a public church. It corresponds closely to the third Epistle of Saint John to Gaius, which is certainly a private letter. The opening of the second Epistle reads: "The presbyter to the Elect Lady and to her children whom I love in truth." The opening of the third Epistle reads: "The presbyter to the beloved Gaius, whom I love in truth."

The second Epistle of Saint John goes on to warn the "Elect Lady" and her community against false teachers, and it ends with greetings from the children of her sister elect. We can understand this sister to be an "Elect Lady" over another community in her house as has been shown was usual in apostolic times.

There is evidence of other women heads of Christian meetings in the letters of Pliny the Younger, the nephew by adoption of Pliny, the author of *Natural History*. The letters were written to Trajan while Pliny the Younger was governor of Bithynia.[8] He said he found it necessary to torture two maids called *ministrae* by the Christians in order to obtain information from them.

They were evidently singled out from among the others as being the ones responsible for the meetings and as being leaders in service of the others.

Many women are known to have been heads of double communities of men and women in early Christian times,[9] both on the Continent and in England, such as the well-known case of Hilda of Whitby.[10] The position of these women heads of communities was similar to that of the women of apostolic times who looked after groups in their own homes and to the "Lady Elect" head of the Christian community in her house addressed by Saint John.

The subject of study in this book—the quasi-episcopal abbesses —can be looked on likewise as continuing the accepted custom of apostolic times. A great number of communities headed by abbesses with independent jurisdiction exempt from bishops were spread throughout Italy, Spain, France, Germany, Poland, Austria, England, and Ireland.

We can conclude that to have women overseers (*episcopae*) [11] of churches and Christian communities was a common practice from apostolic times and that it continued throughout many centuries and was only very slowly suppressed.

CHAPTER TWO
"STONES WILL CRY OUT"

"And some of the pharisees from among the multitude said to him, rebuke thy disciples. To whom he said I say to you that if these shall hold their peace the stones will cry out."

Luke 19:39–40

THE WORD *episcopa*, that is, *bishop* applied to women, is to be found on stone and mosaic inscriptions. These are stones that today cry out truths that have been hidden away. These inscriptions prove that women once held a place in the hierarchical service of the Church that is now denied to them.

In the Church of Saint Praxedis, Rome, there is a mosaic with the word *Episcopa* over the head of a veiled woman, and with the name Theodo(ra) down the side. The name has been tampered with and appears as Theodo. But the head is the head of a woman.

The Church of Saint Praxedis was one of the very earliest titulus churches where bishops presided and where baptisms were performed, although in early times baptism was only given in cathedrals. Wherever baptism was performed deaconesses were necessary for woman catechumens.

The mosaic in question is inside the chapel built by Pope Paschal I in the ninth century in honor of Saint Zeno. Other mosaics in the church are known to date from the fifth century. The later mosaics have been well blended with the earlier ones. The mosaic of the episcopa Theodora depicts the busts of the two sisters Saint Praxedis and Saint Pudentiana, the daughters of Pudens. The church was built on the territory inherited by the sisters from their father.

So we see that as in the East so also in the West, church communities were allocated in the homes of women. It is to be expected that Saint Praxedis would be an "elect lady," like the person addressed by Saint John. The name of overseer, that is, *episcopa*, may well have been passed down from her time.

The mosaic shows Saint Praxedis and Saint Pudentiana on either side of the Virgin Mary. All three have a round halo. To the left of the group is the bust of Theodora with a square halo, which indicates that she was still alive when the mosaic was made, but shows that she held an honorable position. The word *episcopa* is written horizontally above and the name Theodora vertically by the side of the veiled woman.

De Rossi made a thorough examination of the mosaic.[1] He did not consider the horizontal position of the word *episcopa* characteristic of early centuries; he surely was hoping to declare the inscription a late insertion. But he was honest enough to admit that the mosaic cubes were old with a few modern ones put under the name Theodo where the –ra had been eliminated.

The title *Theodora episcopa* is repeated in an inscription on a marble slab on one of the columns outside the chapel. It is a long inscription giving all the names of saints whose relics had been placed by Pope Paschal I in the church. This took place on July 20, 818 according to the *Liber Pontificale*.[2] In this list Theodora episcopa is said to be the mother of Pope Paschal and buried in the church. The mosaic shows Theodora when alive, and she is veiled in white without any jewelry as worn by the senator Puden's daughters.

The question now can be asked whether the mosaic represents the mother of Paschal or an earlier leader of a women's community in service of the titulus church. The list of virgins that follows the name of episcopa Theodora among the inscriptions gives one the impression of being *ancillae Dei*, that is, dedicated

5

virgins. Pope Paschal's mother might well have retired as a widow to head such a community. This does not eliminate the possibility that the mosaic represents an earlier Theodora because there is a mention of a Theodora [3] who came from Alexandria to Rome and who brought relics of saints with her. These were first placed in via Portuense and later transferred by her to the Church of Saint Passera, that is, a variation of the name Praxedis, to whom she was devoted. This was at the time of Pope Innocent I (402–417). There is an epitaph dated 449 in the crypt of the Church of Saint Praxedis with the words *Puella virgo sacra B.M. Alexandria.* So it is possible that Theodora of Alexandria brought a community with her of which she was overseer, that is, *episcopa.*

It is quite well known that the Church of Saint Praxedis was one of the earliest titulus churches in Rome, which may even have dated from apostolic times. If Saint Pudentiana and Saint Praxedis were the daughters of Pudens mentioned by Saint Paul,[4] as is possible, then the church would date from only one generation after Saint Paul.

There are other examples of women bishops. An *episcopa Terni* is mentioned in canon 20 of the Council of Tours, which is reproduced in the *corpus inscriptionis* of Le Blant and also referred to by Grossi-Grandi in his book on Christian epigraphs [5] In the same Council of Tours, canons 13 and 14, deaconesses and subdeaconesses are mentioned.

An *episcopa* is listed in a Vatican Library manuscript taken from an epitaph from the cemetery of the Basilica of Saint Valentiniane.[6] The inscription reads: *(Hono)rabilis femina episcopa.*

The way in which some consecrated widows are recorded also resembles the formulas used by bishops. They are said "to sit in a basilica." The following is an example taken from Marini: [7]

RIEXEM PPLI ANNV
VIDVA SEDIT
BASILICA ASEVISV · RAVIT QUE OBIT EST

There is an interesting epitaph of a widow who is said to be loved by all churches, and it reminds one of the "Elect Lady" of Saint John "whom all who love the truth love."

QUARTA · HIC VIDVA VIXIT. ANN
LXXX · MARCELLINVS KARISSIMVS
FRATER · KARISSIMAE SORORI
ET · PIENTISSIMAE · MERTAE FECIT
QUEM · OMNIS · ECCLESIA · DILIGEBAT.[8]

Not only widows but also deaconesses are said to have served
certain basilicas. For example, at Spolari there is mentioned a
deaconess of the Holy Church:

ARCAE VERATAE
DIAC · SCE ECCLESIAE.[9]

There were a great number of women in the Order of Widows
and Virgins in Rome in A.D. 260 consecrated to the divine mys-
teries, vouched for by Tillemont. He cites fifteen hundred widows in a letter of Pope Cornelius and quoted by Thlibomenis.[10]
John Chrysostom says widows and virgins in the Church of
Antioch amounted to three thousand and more.[11] And we know
by the legislation of the Code of Justinian that the number of
deaconesses at the Basilica of Hagia Sofia alone was not to exceed
forty, as against one hundred deacons.[12] There were many deaconesses also in the West. However, when deaconesses lived in
community they became known as canonesses, that is, they lived
under a rule. The title *deaconess* is therefore less often referred
to. The canonesses were divided into secular and regular canonesses. The seculars lived in private apartments; the regulars lived
in community. They were both in the service of cathedrals or
churches.

It has been shown and proved that women participated in the
administration and services of the Church. It cannot be concluded, however, that they consecrated the Eucharist. The reason
has already been given as due to the idea of the ritual impurity
of women during menstruation, which was an idea held by many
nations.[13]

An exception may have been made for burial services accompanied by the Eucharistic service. Women in pre-Christian times
and in the Christian era have always been to the fore in funeral
celebrations. It was considered their special duty.[14] The fresco
Fractio Panis in the Cappella Greca of the Catacombs of Priscilla

in Via Salerio Nova, Rome, shows a group of women conducting a Eucharistic banquet. The figure to the left is evidently the chief celebrant. The head looks as though it had been sandpapered down, so that it is not clear whether the figure represents a man or a woman. However, by the length of the dress it can be taken for a woman, for men's dresses were shorter. Two of the women in the middle hold their hands outstretched in a meaningful manner and seem to indicate a concelebration.

The catacomb is one of the most ancient cemeteries of Rome. Its primitive subterranean passages contain tombs of early Christians dating back to the first half of the second century. The catacomb bears the name of the foundress Priscilla, a woman of a senatorial family of the Acilii Glabriones, whose Christian members had a burial chamber there. Manlius Acilius Glabrio was consul in A.D. 91. He was put to death by Domitian, probably for his profession of the Christian faith, to which his descendants are known to have adhered. A large property in Via Saleria belonged to the family, and Priscilla arranged for an adjacent area to be used as a burial place for the Christian community at Rome.

The fresco, *Fractio Panis* undoubtedly depicts a Eucharistic service. It is not just an agape, the meal that followed or preceded the Eucharistic service, for nothing is on the table but the symbols of the Eucharist. There is the basket of loaves recording the miracle of the multiplication of the loaves in the desert, and there are the flasks of water turned into wine recording the miracle at the marriage feast at Cana.

So this fresco may indicate that in special circumstances, such as burial services, women were permitted to consecrate the Eucharist.

Certainly the prayer of ordination of abbesses in the Wisigothic Sacramentary declared that before God there is no discrimination of the sexes and that women, like men, are called to collaborate in the spiritual struggle.[15]

CHAPTER THREE

CANONICAL INSTITUTES
AND RELIGIOUS ORDERS

BEFORE ENTERING into a detailed account of the powers of abbesses holding the jurisdiction of bishops, it is necessary to establish the different types of community-living groups that developed through the centuries. There was the group of persons who served the cathedrals, and there was the group of persons who first as hermits and anchoresses lived apart in desert places and who later came together and formed what is known as religious orders. The first group consisted of elected persons ordained for a special purpose in service of the Church, who for convenience lived together under a rule and became known as canons and canonesses. The second group did not consist of elected persons; they were not ordained to a service in the Church, but of their own free will adopted a life of penance and prayer and sought a special form of perfection with freedom for contemplation.

The group in service of the Church lived round about the *Domus-Ecclesiae*, the house-churches that had developed from the early Christian communities established in the houses of women as already mentioned. The *Domus-Ecclesiae* became the site of the bishops' palaces and the cathedrals, with smaller churches attached. It seems that women were the first to live in community. Saint Peter found a group of widows surrounding Tabitha (Dorcas).[1] Saint Basil interprets this passage in the Acts to mean that she belonged to the Order of the Widows.[2] Canonesses like canons are considered to be of apostolic origin. The Augustinian rule for canonesses was written for women and later adapted to men.[3]

The canonesses could belong to either a Secular Canoness Institute or to a Regular Canoness Institute. Members of Secular Canoness Institutes took no vows; they did not live in a convent but in apartments with between three and four other members. They did not have to eat in community. They were paid prebends; that is, a salary, which in early times was in kind—so much food and so much drink. Later it was paid in money. The superior of a Secular Canoness Institute was an archdeaconess as, for example, at Überwasser.[4] Or, according to George Fabricius,[5] the superior was given the name of *Sacerdos Maxima*, while members who were not superiors were called *sacerdotes*. Regular Canoness Institutes members lived together in a single house and took meals in common. They differed from religious orders by the end that they pursued—the members carried out services to the Church that had always been done by deaconesses: the teaching of religion to women, the running of schools, and the care of the sick. The liturgical service other than baptism performed by women was the celebration of Divine Office, which in early centuries was done in the cathedrals and churches as part of a parochial service.

A good example of a Canoness Institute that had as its chief work the chanting of Divine Office in a church that had the status of a parish church was that of Saint Waudru in Mons, Belgium.[6] It is particularly interesting because it started early in the seventh century and lasted until the French Revolution.

The task of historians would have been much easier had the Canoness Institutes and the Religious Orders remained well apart according to their initial aims. Unfortunately this was not the case. Two very different reasons caused an amalgamation of the two. Members of monastic orders who went into the desert and sought to hide in what was thought to be uninhabited islands unexpectedly found themselves surrounded by natives willing to listen to the Christian message, and the monks and nuns could not do other than serve the people. This happened in Ireland and in Britain, where monks and nuns, such as Saint Patrick and Saint Brigid, founded churches. The other reason that caused the slow elimination of Canoness Institutes in favor of religious orders was due to a policy followed by the hierarchy. Perhaps it was due to the greater insistence on the celibacy of priests that it was thought desirable to have canonesses cloistered in the way usual in the purely contemplative orders, and that canonesses should no longer be required to function in parishes or cathedrals but only in their own private chapels or churches.

The canonesses, naturally enough, resisted these new regulations in many places. The canonesses of Saint Mary's Überwasser refused on three occasions to be reformed; they resisted the imposition of the Benedictine Rule on them as they held a completely different vocation.[7] They eventually gave way and then became extinct. The canonesses of Saint Waudru, on the contrary, managed to maintain their rights up to the eighteenth century. In the Annals de Hainaut by Jacques de Guise there is a miniature illustrating the way the clergy, who attempted to eject the canonesses from their choir stalls in the Collegiate and Parish Church of Saint Waudru, were themselves ejected.

In the twelfth century the Counts of Hainaut took over the office of abbot of Saint Waudru, a post which from the seventh century had been held by elected abbesses. The canonesses appealed to the Holy Roman Emperor, but without any success. The counts as abbots held the right to allocate the prebends to persons of their own choice. Some of the prebends were given wrongly to canons instead of to canonesses. Count Régnier of Hainaut, instigated by Cardinal de Sancta Maria in Via Lata, sought to replace all the canonesses by canons. One morning when the canonesses arrived at the entrance of the Church of Saint Waudru they found the door closed, and canons inside had already intoned the introit of the Mass. But they mistakenly were singing the Common of the Martyrs, instead of the Proper of Saint Vincent, which was correct on that day. The canonesses forthwith from outside the church intoned the correct chant.

The Count thereupon changed his mind and sided with the women, for he realized they were more precise in maintaining the liturgical regulations. He turned out the canons and permitted the canonesses to take their place.[8]

According to Ernest Matthieu,[9] in two other places in Belgium the clergy succeeded in turning out the canonesses. In Italy, men and women, both said to be *sacerdotes*, recited the Divine Office together in the Cathedral at Monza.[10] Later this was not allowed. In twelfth-century Milan, at the time of the existence of the dual cathedrals, the canonesses of Sancta Dei Genetrix were removed from a house close to the second cathedral, Santa Maria Maggiore, and they changed their name to the order of Santa Radegunda.[11] It is clear from a letter of Archbishop Galdinus, who insisted on *only* the *clergy* of Santa Maria Maggiore having the right to say Divine Office and sit in the choir stalls, that the canonesses had done so earlier as members of the *decumani* of the cathedral. The *decumani* instituted by Saint Ambrose originally were clerical and included women; but in the letter of Galdinus the *decumani* are said not to be clerical. At one time the canonesses certainly served the women's baptistery of Santo Stefano al Fonte, situated behind the Cathedral of Santa Maria Maggiore, while there was a second baptistery for men at San Giovanni Baptista behind the earlier Cathedral of Saint Tecla. Although the site of the dual cathedrals was only excavated in 1943–44, very few people know about it, and it is kept somewhat hidden. The canonesses of Sancta Maria Genetrix became the Benedictine Nuns of Santa Radegonda, that is, they were forced to change their vocation from one of service to the Church to that of a contemplative order.

The way of life of hermits and anchoresses was a very different vocation from that of the canons and canonesses. Although they lived in community as protection against bandits, they maintained the solitude of the desert by rules of silence. The ideal of detachment from the world was widespread. Already in the fourth century, Palladius gives the number of women in the desert as twenty thousand nuns as against ten thousand monks.[12] History has been falsified by all the emphasis put on the Desert Fathers.

Although neither monks nor nuns were ordained persons, from very early times the monastic leaders were ordained. For example, the deaconess Marthana ruled over the cells of both men and women ascetics who settled around the memorial of Saint Tecla of Seleucia in fourth-century Asia Minor. This information is given by an eyewitness, Etheria, in her account of her pilgrimage through Egypt, Palestine, and Asia Minor.[13] She wrote a daily description of her journey. The shrine of Saint Tecla, she tells us, was situated fifteen hundred paces outside the city of Seleucia. There was a church with numberless cells of men and women. There she found her very dear friend, a holy deaconess, named Marthana, who was ruling over the cells of the *apoctitae* and virgins. The cells were on a hill in the midst of a great wall for protection against robbers.

The site has been excavated by Ernest Herzfeld, Joseph Keil, and Adolf Wilhem.[14] Their findings confirm Etheria's account.

Dating from the fifth century, the Wisigothic Sacramentary gives instructions for the ordination of abbesses. In the prayer it is stated that before God there is no discrimination of the sexes and that women, like men, are called to collaborate in the spiritual struggle.[15] They were invested with sacerdotal robes, the pallium, and the miter. In the Sacramentary of the Moisac Monastery the rite for the abbots and abbesses was identical. They prostrated before the altar and received the stole.

It was very common in both the East and the West for women to be leaders of double communities of monks and nuns.[16] It would be difficult to explain such a novelty if it were not an apostolic tradition arising from the women overseers, if not from the direct teaching of Our Lord himself, for he was accompanied by a group of women who provided for him and his apostles out of their own money.[17] Eight women together with his mother are named as followers of Jesus in Galilee and as present at the Passion.[18]

The position of women as leaders of double communities has sometimes been hidden. For example, the Basilian Order was not founded by Saint Basil but by his sister Macrina. It was she who persuaded Basil to abandon the glory of the world. For four years he lived a monastic life under her guidance, giving himself to working on the land and toiling with his hands. According to the brotherly remark of Gregory of Nyssa, this was necessary in order that Basil overcome his puffed-up pride after finishing his studies at the School of Athens.[19] After the death of her father, Macrina likewise persuaded her mother to join the community and to give up her servants and slaves in order to live at the same standard as they did, undertaking manual work, which was so much despised in countries of Greek culture.

Nevertheless, first place was given to the chanting of Divine Office, the *Laus Perennis*, celebrated night and day without intermission by a sequence of a group of nuns, restricted generally to the number of twelve persons. This was common practice in both the East and the West.

There is an astounding letter from Gregory of Nazianzus to Gregory of Nyssa on the occasion of the death of Theosebia, revealing her as holding a very high office in the Church. Gregory of Nazianzus calls her "the glory of the Church, adornment of Christ, the helper of our generation, the hope of women." She is further said to be truly sacred, a consort of a priest and of equal honor to him, worthy of the Great Sacraments.[20]

The meaning of this letter has been greatly discussed. The reference to Theosebia as a consort of a priest has been taken to mean that she was the wife of Gregory of Nyssa. It was usual, however, for a wife to retire into a convent when her husband entered Holy Orders, although it could be that this regulation was not in force as early as the fourth century. It may be that Theobesia held an important place in the Church at Nyssa as Theodora Episcopa did at the Church of Saint Praxedis in Rome. The fact that she is said worthy of the Great Sacraments is held by some to mean that she could consecrate the Eucharistic species, because the word *sacraments* is in the plural.

It is possible that Theosebia held a position as *co-episcopa* as Saint Brigid of Kildare did in Ireland. For although, according to her biographer Cogitosus, Brigid was ordained bishop by Bishop Mel, she nevertheless called a hermit from his solitary life to govern the Church with her in episcopal dignity.[21] The most probable explanation of such a shared ministry is that as a woman Brigid could not consecrate the Eucharist, at least not until the age of sixty.[22] Perhaps Theosebia at a late age was able to do so considering that she was called worthy of the Great Sacraments.

Other examples of women consecrating the Eucharist are practically nil, but there are indirect proofs that there were some. In a document dated 1756 it is recorded that the canonesses of Saint Waudru had a rule that was destroyed because it made them similar to the Montanists, who consecrated their women as priests and bishops.[23]

The predominance of the monastic ideal and the slow termination of canonical orders for women caused fewer women to be ordained. Only the abbess and possibly one or two members in administration of a religious order would have been ordained; the nuns were consecrated virgins but not ordained. In a canoness order many more members would have been ordained, ordained, that is, at least as deaconess, or archdeaconess, as *sacerdos maxima* as will be seen in the following chapters.

The same predominence of the monastic ideal also affected men, so that secular priests as well as monks were obliged to be celibate. The removal of canonesses from close quarters to the cathedrals to some distance off took place in the twelfth century when celibacy for the priesthood became enforced.

Although ordained canonesses were hampered, it took literally centuries for the tradition to die.

CHAPTER FOUR

THE EPISCOPAL JURISDICTION OF ABBESSES

THERE WAS A CLOSE RELATIONSHIP between the right of queens and the right of abbesses to rule. Queens reigned as co-rulers or as regents or with sole power over their own countries. Abbesses of exempt monastic orders had jurisdiction over their separated districts in both ecclesiastical and civil matters. The mother-right of queens and empresses to rule as regents for their young sons was usually accepted throughout all historical periods, in both the East and in the West. In the Byzantine Empire empresses were co-rulers with the emperors, as, for example, Pulcheria with Marcian and Theodora with Justinian.[1] The empresses were often regents for their sons, as Irene was for Constantine VI. Empresses could also reign in their own right, as Irene did at a later period. During their reigns empresses were able to depose and elect patriarchs, legislate in both ecclesiastical and civil matters, and convoke both local and general councils of the Church.[2] In the West the Ottonian empresses and princesses continued the Byzantine tradition.

The abbesses of royal abbeys had the same position and power as the queens and empresses. The abbeys of the Middle Ages did not consist of a single convent building situated in an enclosed garden as today. The women's abbeys, in the same way as the men's abbeys, depended on the revenues of large territories. These included villages and towns, arable land and rural districts, which the abbesses were obliged to look after and to legislate for by means of civil and ecclesiastical courts.

The quasi-episcopal jurisdiction of an abbess or an abbot did not comprise the sacerdotal powers of a bishop. Such functions as the ordaining of priests, the dedication and consecration of altars, the blessing of the chrismatory oils were reserved to the specific sacerdotal power of the bishop alone. Jurisdiction was considered as another matter, which could be undertaken by abbots and abbesses. The heads of religious orders were not originally selected from persons who had been ordained priests. Neither Saint Benedict nor Saint Francis are considered to have been in Sacred Orders. Nevertheless, superiors of religious orders were "overseers" of their own districts, and as such they had what was later termed "quasi-episcopal" prerogatives.

The monastic freedom and exemption from taxes on their territories paid to the civil powers or from tithes paid to bishops threw the responsibility for raising income on the heads of exempt religious orders, so that they had to undertake certain forms of jurisdiction over their own domains. The right of abbesses to this form of jurisdiction was not questioned until about the time of the Council of Trent. Earlier there had been a considerable amount of litigation between religious orders and bishops concerning the right of religious orders—both monks and nuns—to take the tithes paid by the people on their territories, which otherwise would have gone to the bishops. Religious orders, however, had held their privileges from time immemorial and were unwilling to lose them.

The status of abbesses was undermined at the Council of Trent by the bishops—from whose authority the abbesses were exempt —being given the right to act as delegates of the Holy See; so although nominally not contravening the agelong jurisdiction of the abbesses, the bishops were, in fact, permitted to interfere.[3]

From very early times it was an accepted custom that monks and nuns should be exempt from tithes or taxes. The Church protected those who withdrew from society to live a life of penance

and prayer as having chosen the "better part": a life of medita-
tion sanctioned by Our Lord himself when in favor of Mary he
refused to concede to the demands of Martha.

Already in 672 in England, at the Synod of Hertford, Theodore, Bishop of Canterbury, established in canon 3 of his Penitential that "it shall not be lawful for any bishop to disturb in
any matter any monastery dedicated to God, nor remove by
force any of their possessions." [4] That is to say, men's and wom-
en's religious orders were already independent of the bishop of
the diocese with regard to their way of life and their property.
Archbishop Theodore was appointed to Canterbury by Pope
Vitalian in the second half of the seventh century. Theodore was
a Greek monk and so must have been familiar with both Eastern
and Western customs. The fact that this canon on the exemption
of religious orders was third on the list shows that it was considered important.

The exemption of monasteries can be traced back to a much
earlier date than the seventh century. In a bull sent by Pope
John IV (641) to the Parthenon of *Beatae Mariae et Sanctae
Columbae et Agathae* [5] the exemption, we are led to understand,
was based on a custom practiced during the time of Saint An-
thony, Saint Pachomius, and Saint Benedict Abbot. The Council
of Carthage (525), in canon 2, gave the monasteries the absolute
right to be independent, adding that they always had been so. [6]
At the General Council of Carthage (536), with 217 bishops
present, the right of the independence of monasteries was likewise affirmed. Bishops were requested by the Holy See to ordain
the clergy of the monasteries, but only when the consent of the
abbot or abbess was given. The bishops were not permitted to
receive any contribution for services rendered nor to interfere
in the election of the abbot or abbess. The episcopal chair was
not to be erected in the abbey church except on the occasion of
the dedication of the church or when the bishop was invited for
a special feast day. This was likewise the ruling for the women's
community founded by Cassian at Marseilles and headed by the
Abbess Respecta, as is affirmed in a letter to her from Pope
Gregory the Great. [7]

The Council of Chalcedon required agreement between the religious orders and the bishops. At the Council of Arles (455), however, the power of Bishop Frégus was curtailed and the greater authority given to the abbot of Lérin.

The Celtic Church in Ireland, Britain, and Brittany gave pre-eminence to abbots and to abbesses over bishops as at Iona and Kildare.[8]

At the Council of Agde (506) there was a swing back to the recognition of the predominance of the bishop over the abbots. However, not long afterward, Pope Hormisdas (514–26) gave exemption to the women's community at Arles at the request of Bishop Caesarius, brother of the Abbess Caesaria, the foundress of the Order.[9]

It was Pope Gregory the Great who established exemption of religious orders as the normal custom in the West. He first gave it to Benedictine communities and then to other orders. It is certain that Gregory the Great gave exemption to women's orders as well as to men's, as we have a copy of his letter addressed to Respecta, abbess of the Cassian foundation in Marseilles.[10] The letter confirms an earlier bull of Pope Virgilius giving the community exemption from the jurisdiction of the bishops. The letter required that the abbess be elected from among the nuns and not from persons outside the community, and it stipulated that the abbess be elected by the nuns and hence not appointed by an outside authority as often happened. It added that the elected abbess should be *ordained* by the bishop. The word *ordained* is translated by later writers as *blessed*, thus showing prejudice against the ordination of women. But in earlier centuries the word *ordained* was used for the consecration of abbesses. The abbesses were often deaconesses or archdeaconesses[11] and were sometimes given the title *Sacerdos Maxima*.[12]

Neither the bishop nor any ecclesiastic was to have any power over the Cassian community; its monastery appertained solely to the abbess. On the day of dedication of the monastery—then named in honor of Saint Cassian, although later it was called the Monastery of Saint Savior—the Mass was to be celebrated solemnly by the bishop, but afterward his chair was to be removed from the church of the monastery, corresponding to the regulations made in Africa.[13] The original letter is not extant, and we have only a copy. The injunction that the bishop should choose the priest to serve the Order seems to be in contradiction to the foregoing requirement that the bishop's chair must be removed. It is permissible, therefore, to consider the phrase regarding the bishop making the choice of the priest, as a possible interpolation.

During the Middle Ages there was a big growth of monastic freedom. Not only the abbots and abbesses and their communities were exempt from the bishops' authority, but the secular clergy serving them and the laity within the village churches belonging to the monasteries [14] were also included in the exemption. The religious orders were exempt from the service and taxes due to the king or nobleman and from the tithes due to the bishop. The monasteries of nuns with their clergy and people were directly dependent on the Holy See.

The effect of these exemptions was to give the abbesses as well as the abbots a position of quasi-episcopal jurisdiction; that is, they had the same duties and rights to act within their separated territories belonging to the congregation as had a bishop within his diocese. The right of jurisdiction was quite independent of the power of the priesthood, as already mentioned. In the later Middle Ages a more definite terminology was developed, and the abbesses, like the abbots, were established as of *Nullius Diocesis* and as *Praelatura Nullius, qualitate nullius,* with both spiritual and temporal jurisdiction recognized by many papal bulls through numerous centuries. The last abbess to hold this position was the Abbess Bernarda Ruiz Puente of Las Huelgas of Burgos, Spain, with twelve dependent convents holding the same privileges, whose right of jurisdiction was abolished in 1874.[15]

The books that have been published on the subject of monastic freedom have been chiefly concerned with men's orders.[16] There were, in fact, many women's orders with the privilege of exemption and directly dependent on the Holy See. If one takes the Register of Pope Gregory IX alone, which has the advantage of being considered completely authentic, there are numerous examples of women's orders that were given exemption from the bishop and made directly dependent on the Holy See.

The exemption consisted as a form of protection against either ecclesiastical or civil encroachment on the territories of the monasteries. In many cases it was the donor, generally, a member of a feudal family, who requested the papal protection, so that the gift would not finish up in wrong hands. Often the bishop's agreement was also sought and given, for it was not necessarily against the bishop's interest to have lucrative neighbors who took over some of the burden of looking after parishes, which he had not the means to run so well. Sometimes it was the bishop himself, as in the case of Bishop Caesarius of Arles, who asked the pope for this form of protection, knowing the perils these monasteries faced. As time went on, and the papacy itself became stronger, popes were asked more and more frequently to give this papal protection. But the popes became more reluctant to give the privilege unless the order could prove that the right of exemption had been given in the past from "time immemorial." This led to many monasteries hunting up old documents, many of which had been lost in invasions and fires and other disasters, and alleged copies were made, which later historians have considered forgeries. Such accusations have been made sometimes too easily. There is no doubt that these privileges were common. Gregory the Great gave the right of exemption to all Benedictine monasteries, Gregory IX to all houses of the Order of Saint Clare, and Alexander III to all houses of the Order of Fontevrault. The following examples, taken from the Register of Gregory IX, give some idea of how widespread was the custom in many different countries: [17]

No.406.[18] The pope confirms the privileges given earlier by Honorius III to the abbess and nuns of Sancta Maria extra Portam Sensensen de Camulia, in protection against Hugo, Bishop of Ostia and Velletra, who is stated (in an attached letter) to have no right over the monastery as it is dependent on the Holy See.

No.105.[19] Gregory IX renews the privileges already given by Pope John, Pope Leo, and Innocent III to Abbess Sophia and the nuns of Sanctae Mariae et Petri et Sancti Cyriarci in Gernode; the community and all its possessions are taken under protection of the Holy See.

No.445.[20] Confirmation of the papal exemption was given to Abbess Hersende of the Abbey of Jouarre, and of her community, clergy, and people, declaring them independent of the jurisdiction of the Archbishop of Sens.

No.5267.[21] The prioress of the Convent of Halliwell, London, of the Order of Saint Augustine, whose jurisdiction over the Church of Welleswes was given earlier by Hugo of Lincoln, has her rights confirmed.

No.5274.[22] Regarding a disagreement of the Abbess of Fontevrault with the Bishop of Poitou, who sought to make an episcopal Visitation, the abbey is confirmed independent from the jurisdiction of the bishop.

No.5349.[23] The Abbey of Fontevrault is again confirmed as not being under the jurisdiction of the diocese of Poitou.

No.6000.[24] All the abbesses and nuns of the Order of Saint Damian are declared exempt from episcopal jurisdiction.

The letter of Gregory IX to the Abbess Audisia of Brundisio (Brindisi) [25] is long and very interesting because it shows that a Benedictine women's community had enormous territories with many churches dependent on it. This exempt abbey had existed a long time before the arrival of the Cistercian women's community that took over the property of the monks of Saint Benedict at Conversano.[26] The transfer of the right of exemption is considered by some writers a terrible abuse. Had the Cistercian nuns taken over the Benedictine women's monastery at Brindisi, they would have had a far greater district to rule and many more churches, priests, and laity under their jurisdiction than at Conversano. The bull of Gregory IX (March 15, 1233) gives the full list of the villages, churches, and property belonging to the Brindisi community. It confirms the privileges given earlier by Paschal II (1099–1118), Callixtus II (1119–24), Honorius II (1124–30), Alexander III (1159–81), and Celestine III (1191–98), predecessors of Gregory IX. There were some thirty-six churches, and it is interesting to note that in them both Greek and Latin rites were allowed, for the whole of Apulia, in which Brindisi is located, had come under Greek domination at various periods in history, while at other times it had been included under the rule of Naples.

The abbesses were given both spiritual and temporal jurisdiction. In a letter to the abbess of the Monastery of Saint Mary and Saint Apollinarius-Outside-the-Gates of-Rome in Milan, Saint Gregory states it explicitly: they have exemption: *ab omni episcopali, et cujuslibet, conditionis obligatione tam temporalibus quam in spiritualibus pleno jure liberamus.* And, moreover, any excommunication of the order by the bishop is declared invalid. This clause was included in many bulls.[27]

CONCLUSION

This survey gives some idea of the growth of monastic exemption and of the great number of women's monasteries that held independent jurisdiction. It gives an idea of what this jurisdiction entailed: abbesses with independent jurisdiction had all the duties of a bishop with regard to ecclesiastical and civil administration in a diocese, which in their case was called a "separated territory." The abbesses had spiritual and temporal jurisdiction, which in Canon Law was termed *nullius diocesis* or *praelatura nullius.* This status did not entail a priestly ordination, even though abbesses had a form of ordination.

Owing to the great number of independent monasteries governed by quasi-episcopal abbesses it has not been possible in this volume to give a really comprehensive survey. A few examples have been selected from the different countries, which show how universal a custom this form of jurisdiction became. It was considered based on a tradition of "immemorial" existence.

CHAPTER FIVE

EXEMPT WOMEN'S
ORDERS IN ENGLAND

A LTHOUGH THERE ARE quite a number of documents showing that women's orders in England were exempt from the
jurisdiction of bishops in the same way as on the Continent, there is very little literature on the subject. Of course,
the fact that monasteries were all dissolved in the sixteenth century was the cause of the loss of many documents; besides, the
registration made at the time of the dissolution by persons hostile
to the existence of religious orders produced prejudiced and
scanty information.

The best known community headed by Saint Hilda at Whitby,
then called Streanaeshalch, was of Celtic tradition. Like Saint
Tecla's memorial in Seleucia, the community consisted of hermits
and anchoresses living around a communal church. Hilda saw to
the formation of the clergy, for we are told by Bede [1] that it was
due to her insistence that the clergy, many of whom subsequently became bishops, received training in the Holy Scriptures.
In her community no one was rich or poor, for everything
was held in common, and none possessed personal property.
The church and community buildings stood on a hill overlooking the bay at the mouth of the river Eask. The archeo-

logical site has been studied by Charles Peers and Ralegh Radford.[2]

The community must have been of considerable size, as traces of the structure extend three hundred feet east and west, and nearly two hundred feet northwest with no signs of a boundary. In 1078, some two hundred years after the destruction of Hilda's settlement by the Danes, the writer of the cartulary of the subsequent Benedictine men's abbey built on the same site mentions that there were still forty roofless oratories or cells standing around the church of Saint Peter, in which the Mercian king's tombs had been interred. The importance of Hilda's foundation can be judged by the fact that it was chosen to be the place for the meeting of the Church Council regarding the retention of the Celtic liturgy or the adoption of the new Roman rites. Hilda would most certainly have taken part in the discussions of the Council as did her successor, Abbess Aelfleda, at the Synod of Nidd.[3] Aelfleda was called the counselor of the whole province.

Bede[4] wrote a good description of the monastery at Coldingham, which was headed by Ebba, who was called *Sacerdos Maxima*[5] by Fabricius. Here again there were many private cells around a church center. It was at Coldingham that Queen Etheldreda, later to become *Sacerdos Maxima* of Ely, took the veil.[6]

People of all ages and social levels came to Ely to live under Etheldreda's direction. Sexburga, Etheldreda's widowed sister, joined her and continued, after Etheldreda's death, to govern in the same way. Sexburga was followed by her daughter, Erminilda, likewise a widow. Erminilda was followed, in turn, by her daughter, Werburga, who at an early age became a *Sponsa Christi* and is said to have had the custody of the church.[7] The *Liber Eliensis* records that after the death of these four great abbesses, the monastery continued as before in ever greater fervor under the *beatarum regimine ferminarum*,[8] until the time of the Danish invasion in 866.

It is known that during the lifetime of Etheldreda, Bishop Wilfrid went to Rome to obtain a papal privilege for her foundation.[9] When he returned with it in 679, Saint Etheldreda had died, and Sexburga was abbess. Although we do not have the document, we know that in 672 Archbishop Theodore had already laid down that "it was not lawful for any bishop to disturb in any matter any monastery dedicated to God." [10] We can assume that the privilege was the usual one of exemption from the jurisdiction of bishops, especially since the Ely foundation was under Benedictine rule, and Pope Gregory I gave exemption to the Benedictine order in general, which is known to have included women's houses. [11]

Another early example of the independent status of women's monasteries in the seventh and eighth centuries is the privilege granted by King Wihtred of Kent to religious orders in general at the Council of Beccanceld in 694. Five abbesses of foundations in Thanet, Dover, Folkestone, Lyming, and Sheppey were present and signed the decrees after the archbishops, but before all other clergy present. [12]

A number of papal bulls giving exemption to the Abbey of Wherwell have been preserved for us in the British Museum. [13] The abbey was founded about 986 by Elfrida, queen dowager of King Edgar, to expiate the murder of her first husband, Ethelwolfe, committed to enable her to become queen, and to ensure the accession of her son as king. Ethelred gave the abbey exemption from all earthly services, and endowed it with the gift of many territories and churches. [14]

The papal bulls date from a much later time, but we see by the bull of Gregory IX, in the second year of his Pontificate (1228), that the abbey still had dependent churches and possessions. This bull has been printed by Dugdale. [15]

The churches and places dependent on the abbey listed in the bull, together with the exact amount each had to contribute, gives an idea of the extent of the abbey's ecclesiastical possessions. These were: the Church of Holy Cross and Saint Peter's of Wherwell; the Trinity Church and chapel of Saint Mary's and Saint Michael; Saint Peter's Church of Codewirdâ; the Church of Saint Nicolas of Middleton; the Church of Blessed Mary of Bolyndione with its manors; the Church of Saint Nicholas of Compton; the Church of Blessed Mary of Wycâ and Wlleghe; the Church of Blessed Mary at Colynghburna and the manors therewith; the Church of Saint Peter's of Everle; the Church of Saint Martin in the city of Winton with the manor: The right to certain woods, villas, and manors are likewise listed; and the right to the *decima* of the churches of Tokynton, Wingemarese, Bromley, the parish churches of Newchurche, and two parts of the *decima* of Bradfield, and all the *decima* of Drayton, and a third of the *decima* of Chelewarton.

The benediction of the nuns at their profession was to be given by the diocesan bishop "*gratis et sine praevitate aliqua*"; that is, gratis and without any conditions in the same way as at Fontevrault,[16] Burgos, and other exempt women's monasteries in Europe. The bull of Gregory IX ends with the usual declaration that nobody may disturb the community nor its possessions, which are to be preserved in their integrity and governed by the abbey with juridical rights, except in those things reserved to the Holy See and the canonical juridical rights of the diocesan bishops. These consisted in the right to consecrate the churches and altars and the holy chrismal oils (a yearly concession of which was allowed to the abbeys), the benediction of the abbesses, and the giving of the veil to nuns.[17]

The other papal documents contained in Egerton MS 2104a are confirmations of the same privileges given by Gregory IX and Alexander IV (fol 18v-20r) and a second bull from the same pope. Innocent III, in the second year of his pontificate, confirmed the same privileges and added regulations regarding the *decima* of other churches, that is, Walhop etc. Another bull from Gregory IX, in the ninth year of his pontificate (f. 23r), also concerned the payment of the *decima;* Pope Celestine and Pope Alexander X again confirmed these privileges.

It is known by the evidence given of the many European exempt monasteries with quasi-episcopal abbesses that this right was more particularly allowed to royal abbeys, such as the Royal Abbey of Jouarre, the Royal Abbey of Fontevrault, the Royal Abbey of Conversano, and the Royal Abbey of Las Huelgas at Burgos. In the Domesday Book, abbesses of nine nuns' houses are said to be held from the king;[18] that is, they were also royal abbeys, and we can expect them to have powers similar to those of the royal abbeys on the Continent.

Shaftesbury Abbey was a royal abbey founded by Alfred the Great for his daughter, Ethelgeofu. It was built in 888 on the site of a former monastery destroyed by the Danes. Tanner, quoted by Dugdale, lists the abbesses as controlling several prebends of secular priests [19] in Ywern and Gillingham in Dorsetshire, and in Ladington and Fontell in Wiltshire. These churches were therefore *Eigenkirche*—a word coined by the Germans to denote the churches possessed by privileged monasteries that did not belong to a diocese. However, Shaftesbury could not have been exempt for long, as at an early date chaplains dependent on bishops are mentioned instead of canons, who were dependent on the abbess.

Three large nunneries in the county of Hampshire, Nunnaminster, Wherwell, and Romsey had canons, who in an early period had prebendal stalls in the choir and seats in the Chapter, which shows they were dependent on the abbess. After 1301 the priests serving the monastery were called chaplains rather than canons.[20] This shows a loss of status on the part of the abbess and abbey. The abbess was no longer given the prerogatives of a bishop as was usual to quasi-episcopal abbesses on the Continent. That this right was lost so much earlier in England than in Europe may have been due to greater difficulty of communication with the Holy See.

The Order of Fontevrault retained its privileges longer. The Fontevrault house in Nuneaton received papal bulls on July 23, 1184–85 and again on July 29 in which Lucius III gave the Prioress Hethonia and the nuns exemption from episcopal jurisdiction in the same way as the mother house at Fontevrault in France.[21] The bull of July 29 is very insistent on the rights of the nuns, showing that the house had had some trouble due to their exemption. In this bull the pope renewed the prohibition against archbishops, bishops, deacons, and all ecclesiastical persons taking over the churches or excommunicating the nuns. There are records of the English houses of Fontevrault to be found in the Calendar of the Close Rolls.I. 354–6 and 669–70, and in the bull of Urban VI (1381). The priors of Nuneaton and Westwood were licensed to attend the General Chapter of the Order of Fontevrault in France in May 1344 according to the Calendar of Patent Rolls in 1343–46 (383).[22] This shows that the Fontevrault Houses in England were still exempt, as they had been from their foundation, recognized by a bull of Pope Alexander III.[23] (He was the Pope who gave general exemption to all Fontevrault foundations.) It is stated in the bull that liberty was granted by King Henry II and the bishops. Eleanor of Aquitaine was then queen of England, and we can assume that she arranged this, for she was an enthusiastic and generous benefactor of the Order of Fontevrault.

Other examples of exempt orders in England are known through the bulls of Anastatius IV, who gave papal protection to Matilda, prioress of Nun Coten,[24] reconfirmed by Alexander III. He forbade the archbishops or bishops from prohibiting the nuns from celebrating Divine Office.[25] That the bishops attempted to stop the nuns from celebrating Divine Office shows that at this time there was a movement to eliminate women from the services of the Church.

One of the largest canoness communities with exemption from the jurisdiction of the bishop was that of Saint Mary's Clerkenwell.[26] Pope Urban III took them under papal protection on October 19, 1186, and Pope Celestine III confirmed their rights on October 27, 1194.

The bull of Urban III required the community to follow the Benedictine Rule, but he did not address them as Benedictines, nor does Pope Celestine III. In 1258 the Calendar of Wills of the Court of Husting,[27] London, a minor canon of Saint Paul's, Elys Martin, made a bequest to the *canonesses* of Clerkenwell. Later, again in the Register of Henry Chichele,[28] Archbishop of Canterbury, there were two entries dated 1420 and 1424, in which the Prioress of Clerkenwell, as proprietor of the Church at Sittingborne in Kent, was entitled O.S.A.—the Order of Saint Augustine, which is usual for canonesses. Later writers, after the suppression of the monasteries, have mistakenly called the nuns Benedictines. In the twelfth century there was a general policy to make canonesses come under the monastic rule of Saint Benedict; canons were also encouraged to become regular canons or to enter a monastic order. The canonesses of Saint Mary's Überwasser, in Münster, Germany, rebelled three times against the imposition of the Benedictine Rule on them, which enforced a life of greater separation from the world.[29]

The canonesses of Clerkenwell had property spread over eleven counties around London and sixty-four parish territories within London. Whenever they were granted a church with parochial rights, the deed was witnessed by one or more bishops. The bishops were therefore in favor of the system of parishes being under the care of women's religious orders or institutes. It meant they had the right to the tithes, but that they were also responsible for the maintenance of the churches and for the salaries of the priests. In an act of Henry VIII, the Bishop of London is said to have acquired jurisdiction over Clerkenwell and the parish, which before then had been exempt.[30] Holtzmann mentions several other English communities that were taken under papal protection.[31]

CONCLUSION

There is evidence that between the seventh and ninth centuries, women's religious orders in England held a high position. The abbesses ruled over the clerical and monks' houses as well as the nuns'. Some of the abbesses, according to George Fabricius, had the title of *Sacerdos Maxima*.[32] Most monasteries were completely destroyed during the Danish invasions, although with the revival of monastic life under Alfred the Great some earlier foundations—such as at Wherwell, Romsey, and Barking—were able to continue and maintained an exempt status up to about the fourteenth century. A new and important women's Benedictine royal abbey was started at Shaftesbury. The women's loss of status can be noted by the fact that with the coming of the Normans, the sites of the important women's foundations of earlier times at Whitby, Thanet, and Ely were taken over by men's orders. However, the introduction of Fontevrault houses in England revived the custom of women superiors governing the clergy and monks as well as the nuns. All these women's communities supervised the churches listed among their property; they had the right to the tithes, and they had the duty to maintain the buildings and to provide the salary for the priests.

There were Canoness Institutes[33] besides religious orders in England, of which Saint Mary's Clerkenwell in London was the largest. The superiors were called prioresses rather than abbesses, which shows that they would normally have been dependent on a bishop or a higher superior, and properly speaking should not have been exempt. But the canoness status became so mixed up with that of nuns that canonesses at some period were also given exemption. The bishops accepted the system of women custodians of churches as is seen by the deeds witnessed by bishops.

CHAPTER SIX

QUASI-EPISCOPAL ABBESSES IN FRANCE

THE ROYAL ABBEY OF NOTRE-DAME DE JOUARRE [1]

ODAY THE ABBEY OF NOTRE-DAME DE JOUARRE is one hour's journey by train from Paris and is three miles from the village of Ferté-sous-Jouarre. The nuns still follow the Benedictine Rule, but the abbess no longer holds the quasi-episcopal jurisdiction that the abbesses held in the past.

THE SEVENTH-CENTURY FOUNDATION

In the first decade of the seventh century, a nobleman of Meaux named Chagneric gave hospitality to the Irish monk Saint Columban who founded many monastic centers through Gaul, including one in Bobbio, Italy. It was just after Columban had been expelled from Bobbio for keeping the Celtic date of Easter that, returning through Gaul, he stayed in Chagneric's house, and he blessed Chagneric's infant daughter, Fara, who was to become the foundress of Faremoutier in Brie, not far from Jouarre. Columban then proceeded to Ussy on the Marne, where he stayed with Bishop Autherius and his wife Aiga. At this time it was still common for clergy and bishops to marry. Columban blessed Autherius' two sons, Adon and Dado. Later Adon became one of the founders of the Abbey of Jouarre, and Dado the founder of the men's community connected with Jouarre at Rebais.[2]

According to an ancient document,[3] now no longer in existence, Saint Balde (the sister of Mode, the second wife of Bishop Autherius) was the director behind the scenes of the foundation at Jouarre. Saint Balde arranged for her niece, Teudechild, daughter of her brother Betto, to become the first abbess of Jouarre. Later she arranged for another niece, Aguilberte, daughter of her brother Abobinus, to become the second abbess of Jouarre. Saint Balde herself took vows of obedience to her nieces in turn. It was evidently also through her influence that the brother of Teudechild retired to a place of solitude in Jouarre, once a hide-out for brigands, and there together with others (which may well have included Adon, the son of Autherius and his first wife Aiga) prepare the place as a center of prayer. There Teudechild joined him with a large group of women. Two houses were built, one within the enclosure and the other outside. At first the men took the building inside the enclosure, but on the request of Teudechild the men agreed to take the outside one and the women the inside one, as the latter afforded more protection.

Saint Balde outlived both her nieces, and at a very advanced age became the third abbess of Jouarre by the unanimous election of the community. She died in 680. The tombs of the early founders can still be seen in the crypts of Saint Paul and Saint Ebregesile in the abbey grounds.[4]

After the death of Saint Balde, the names of the abbesses are not known until that of Abbess Ermentrude in 836. The ravages of war caused the loss of a large number of documents, burnt with the buildings that housed them. There has never been any reference to an abbot of Jouarre. In the registers of Pope Clement [5] the canons of Jouarre are said to have had the right to participate in the election of the Abbess of Jouarre, in accordance with a very ancient custom of the abbey. Presumably, therefore, the monks and canons in the outer house of Jouarre must have served the abbey and the church. When the Abbey of Rebais was built at some distance from Jouarre, the monks remained in close relationship with the Abbey of Jouarre.

THE ABBEY BECOMES ROYAL

The Abbess Ermentrude of Jouarre is mentioned as belonging to high rank. She obtained permission from Louis the Pious (778–840) to exchange a territory belonging to the abbey with another belonging to the Abbot of Saint Denis. The fact that she had to get permission from the king shows that the Abbey of Jouarre was then already a royal one,[6] as were the Abbey of Chelles and the Abbey of Faremoutier.

In Carolingian times, Jouarre became an important pilgrimage place on the route between Montmirail and Meaux, due to the many relics gathered by Abbess Ermentrude from the Holy Land, so that people came to pray and to petition for cures. About 859 the abbeys of Jouarre, Chelles, and Faremoutiers obtained royal protection and a confirmation of their exemption from taxes. The exemption, therefore, must have dated from an earlier period. They also had the right to stamp their own coinage.[7] The Abbey of Jouarre followed the Benedictine Rule as well as that of Saint Columban. This was the way that the Benedictine Rule was introduced in many monasteries along side the earlier rule of Saint Columban. As the right of exemption from the bishop was granted to all Benedictine communities by Gregory the Great,[8] there is no reason to suppose that Jouarre was not also independent.

The fame of the Abbey of Jouarre by the twelfth century can be judged by the visit of Pope Innocent II to the abbey on February 25, 1131, while he was traveling through France. In 1133 the abbey was chosen as a place for a council of the Church. This council was to decide the case of the assassination of Thomas of Villeneuve, prior of the Abbey of Saint Victor in Paris.[9] Such a meeting required accommodations for many people, and it entailed much organization, so it denotes that at this time Jouarre must have been very prosperous, and a well-established religious center. It was not the first time that a women's abbey was chosen to be the site for a council of the Church; Saint Hilda's community at Whitby was likewise chosen for a council of the Church in the seventh century.[10]

FIRST LITIGATION BETWEEN THE ABBEY AND THE BISHOPS OF MEAUX. 1128–1225

There was no argument regarding the exemption of the Abbey of Jouarre, until 1128; that is, not until five hundred years after its foundation. Then there arose a litigation between the bishops of Meaux and the abbey that lasted almost a hundred years. These litigations were by no means restricted to the Abbey of Jouarre. Other monasteries were simultaneously prosecuted by the bishops; in particular, the men's Abbey of Rebais was accused together with the women's Abbey of Jouarre as having no right to exemption from the bishop. The right of the Abbess of Jouarre to hold jurisdiction over the people and clergy and members of the community of the Abbey of Jouarre was not contested on the basis of her sex. The idea that a woman could not hold this form of jurisdiction did not arise until the time of Bossuet five hundred years later.

The Bishop Bouchard of Meaux was the first to bring up the question and to contest the right held then by the abbeys of Rebais and of Jouarre over the clergy, churches, and people within their respective territories. Jouarre had certainly held immunity from taxes from Carolingian times; Lemarignier believes exemption was founded on custom not documents in the seventh century.[11] The right of exemption given to the religious communities included the people who were within the territories of the abbeys and clergy serving the churches in their territory. The abbeys were responsible for the prebends of the clergy and for the well being of the laity and, consequently, for the wielding of ecclesiastical and civil justice within the boundaries of their property. Today such an arrangement is looked on by some as an abuse, but in the Middle Ages it was considered a beneficial service.

At first, Pope Honorius II, who was appealed to with regard to the dispute, sided with Bishop Bouchard in a bull addressed to him on April 11, 1125.[12] The pope established that the clergy and laity in the domains of Rebais and Jouarre should be subject to the bishop. The communities of Rebais and Jouarre were also required to be in obedience to the bishop. The fact that the obedience of the community was put separately from that of the clergy and people shows that Honorius considered their position with regard to the bishop in some way different. Although this document is opposed to the independent jurisdiction of the abbeys, it is important as the first documentary evidence that before 1125 the abbeys did hold jurisdiction over clergy and people as well as over the members of the religious communities. Five hundred years later this document was referred to at the time of the lawsuits conducted by Bossuet against Jouarre.

Both abbeys sought to defend themselves by claiming that their rights were based on a long-standing tradition. Naturally enough, as a result of the vicissitudes of wars and climatic disasters documents had been lost; but the abbeys were expected to produce documentary evidence. Rebais claimed to have two bulls: one of Pope John IV [13] (641–42) and one of Pope Martin, I [14] (649–55). Both are judged by scholars today as having been forged in the twelfth century. But the same bulls were judged authentic by Pope Innocent II, who had succeeded Honorius II. The Abbey of Rebais was therefore given papal protection, including the five parishes under its jurisdiction, and granted "Roman liberty."

Jouarre did not venture to fabricate false bulls, but it seems that the bull of Honorius II nevertheless did not come into effect, for at this time Abbess Rissende of Faremoutier also opposed the Bishop of Meaux, Manasses II, who sought to claim the abbey as subject to the diocese. But Abbess Rissende established the tradition of independence of the abbeys of Faremoutier, Rebais, and Jouarre through the fact that according to very ancient custom no clergy from the three communities had ever attended the diocesan synods.[15]

In 1164 there was a reversal of the decision taken on the Abbey of Rebais. Pope Alexander III, by request of Bishop Stephen of Meaux, issued a bull similar to that of Honorius II withdrawing the exemption. Rebais did not give way until excommunicated at the Council of Beauvais in 1168.

Jouarre did not come into this litigation, but the same pontiff, Alexander III, gave Simon I, the Bishop of Meaux, a loophole by which he could interfere in the affairs of the abbey if the election of a new abbess did not take place within a limited time. So when the Abbess Eustache was elected, the bishop brought up the case again. The conflict was settled by a commission of the Archbishop of Rheims, William of Champagne, and the Cardinal legates. The Abbess Eustache was obliged publicly to recognize the authority of the Bishop of Meaux and to promise obedience to him. The bishop performed the ceremony of the installation of the abbess.[16]

The following abbess, Agnes I, refused to take the oath to the Bishop Anseau of Meaux. The clergy and people of Jouarre were fully in agreement with her. Pope Innocent III sent a bull to the Bishop of Paris, Eudes de Sully, dated May 23, 1202,[17] requesting him to bring about the subjection of the Abbey of Jouarre and its clergy and people to the Bishop Anseau of Meaux, and likewise the subjection of the abbot and monks of Rebais. The Abbess Agnes asked for time to find the necessary documents to prove her case, but was refused, and forthwith the abbess and the clergy and the people of Jouarre were excommunicated.[18]

The Abbess Agnes II then made a journey to Rome, accompanied by other members of her community. She took with her decretals proving her right to exemption from the jurisdiction of the bishop. Pope Innocent III was convinced of their authenticity and named a commission to reinstate the abbey together with their clergy and people of Jouarre.[19]

All three abbeys—Jouarre, Rebais, and Faremoutier—based their claim on a privilege given them in 637 by Bishop Faron, the brother of Fara. The original and first copy of the privilege have been lost. The copies kept in the *Bibliothèque de Paris* date from the twelfth century to the thirteenth century, according to the opinion of the *Bulletin de la Société d'archéologie Science, lettres et arts, du département de Seine et Marne*. Pope Honorius III included a copy of the privilege in his bull sent to the Abbey of Jouarre at its request, owing to the poor condition of its copy. This copy was dated Lateran, third of the nones of March, ninth year of the pontificate.[20] And on May 7, 1225 the Abbess Her-

sende was confirmed as exempt and independent of the Archbishop of Sens.[21]

Litigations regarding the right of the Abbey of Jouarre to exemption did not arise again for a period of five hundred years.
Although the copies of the privilege given by Bishop Faron are of
a late date, the contents were quite in keeping with the custom
of the time, since exemption of religious orders was granted from
the time of Gregory the Great.

JOUARRE AND THE REFORMATION

One difficulty was solved but others arose. The Hundred Years
War in France caused much hardship, buildings were burned,
and at one time Jouarre was under military occupation by the
English and Burgundians. The abbey became uninhabitable, and
the community sought protection from the Dauphin. When peace
was made the nuns returned. The documents regarding the exemption of the abbey were again lost, but a confirmation was
wisely obtained in 1461, which was used later at the time of
Bossuet.

In 1516 the diocese of Meaux became the center of the Prot-
estant Reformation in France, and the abbey was also involved.
The Abbess Charlotte de Bourbon, installed at the age of fifteen
(against her own judgment), became convinced of the Lutheran
doctrines through the influence of her sister, Françoise de Bourbon, and sought to introduce the Lutheran faith into the abbey
(1561–72). On not succeeding, she decided to escape from the
abbey. She left France, since she was in danger of her life, and
went to Germany, where she married William of Orange-Nassau
and raised a family.

The abbesses Jeanne de Lorraine and Marie de la Tremoille
undertook a reform of the abbey, which consisted chiefly in a
return to a more exacting spirit of poverty. They eliminated the
lay servant women (it had been the custom for every nun to have
her own private maidservant). The cells of the nuns were simpli-
fied; the dress, which had been white, was changed to a more
penetential black; the grill was covered by a curtain in order to
obtain a greater degree of retirement from worldly affairs.

THE LITIGATION BETWEEN JOUARRE
AND BOSSUET

Jacques Benigne Bossuet (1627–1704) was made Bishop of Meaux in 1681. He sought to destroy the age-long system of the quasi-episcopal jurisdiction of abbots and abbesses within his diocese. He used every means and contrivance to attain his end.

As a boy, until the age of fifteen, he studied with the Jesuits. But already at the age of thirteen he was given a canonry at Metz through the influence of his father. He continued his studies in Paris; in 1652 he was ordained priest and spent seven years at Metz. He entered into the thick of the Lutheran controversy. He became a well-known orator and a prolific writer. There are forty-three volumes of his published works.

Just before being elevated to the bishopric of Meaux, Bossuet was drawn into a controversy with Louis XIV in opposition to Clement X and Innocent XI over a question of the Gallican clergy. Bossuet sought to solve the matter by pursuing a middle course. He drew up a declaration with the consent of the King— *Déclaration du Clergy de France*—in which he tried to establish that the successors of Saint Peter have the right of jurisdiction over spiritual things but not over the temporal goods and property that belong to Caesar. The Gallican clergy considered they had the right to accept or refuse decrees established at Rome with regard to diffusion in France. The Declaration was declared null and void by the pope. The effect of this litigation on Jouarre was to deprive them of protection of the king against Bossuet, as the king could not afford to be at variance with Bossuet. The abbey was likewise deprived of papal protection because the papacy was in a difficult position regarding interference in France.

The method Bossuet used to bring the exempt religious orders situated in his diocesan district under his own jurisdiction was to hold a lawsuit against them on some charge and, with all the dexterity of a competent lawyer, make it necessary for him to interfere in the administration of the community. At first Bossuet brought up a charge of simony against Jouarre. It was a very evidently false one, for he based it on the fact that five hundred years earlier, in 1225, Cardinal Romain had arranged for Jouarre to contribute a certain quantity of grain to the bishop of Meaux as a conciliatory measure, although still leaving the abbey exempt from the jurisdiction of the bishop. Bossuet tried to establish that by this act the Abbey of Jouarre had bought its spiritual exemption and that it was an act of simony. The Abbey of Jouarre defended itself by maintaining that this contribution was not given in exchange for a spiritual benefit, but as a recompense for the temporal benefits the bishops of Meaux world ordinarily receive from religious orders under their jurisdiction.

Bossuet eventually dropped the accusation of simony, and instead accused Jouarre of not having authentic privileges, contradicting the decision of Cardinal Romain in 1225 as an abuse. The lawsuit was conducted in seven sessions. The minutes of the sessions are only known through the account of Bossuet in his *Mémoire sur les moyens de cassation de Mme l'abbesse de Jouarre*.[22] In it he relates that the Abbess Henriette of Lorraine sought to defend herself by affirming that as the abbey was a royal one, it held all the prerogatives normally belonging to royal abbeys. Her counsel for the defense affirmed that ever since the time of the decision taken by Cardinal Romain—that is, for five hundred years—the abbey had enjoyed the rights of jurisdiction over its territory without any trouble. Many proofs were cited. Furthermore, on May 26, 1631, the French Parlement confirmed the abbey's rights. In 1680, the king requested Rome to nominate the Archbishop of Paris as papal delegate for the visitation of the abbey; the pope despatched a brief complying with the king's request. The example of the Abbey of Fontevrault was cited as having maintained its right of jurisdiction when it was likewise attacked by the bishop of Poitiers. It was emphasized that the episcopal jurisdiction of exempt abbeys was quite independent of the power of the priesthood.

But Bossuet continued to maintain that the privileges granted in the documents of Jouarre were not authentic, and he added that even if they were authentic, the ordinances of the councils of Trent and Vienna had revoked them.[23]

The political position already referred to between the papacy and France led the judges to settle in favor of Bossuet on January 26, 1690. The abbess appealed to Rome, but received no answer for two months. Meanwhile, Bossuet acted quickly and dispatched a letter announcing his visitation of the abbey in the following February, one month from the winning of his case.

THE BREAKING OF THE ABBEY DOORWAY BY BOSSUET

True to his word, Bossuet presented himself at the entrance of the town of Jouarre on Saturday, February 25, 1690, together with his vicar general, M. Phelippeaux, and his promoter, M. Corvisart, and his secretary, M. Lideau. The clergy of the town came to meet him in solemn procession. The parish priest, Jacques Bernage, prostrated himself at the feet of Bossuet and handed over his stole, which was then ceremoniously returned, so conveying the priest's subjection to the bishop. The clergy led the bishop to the church amid the inhabitants who thronged the road while there was a festive ringing of bells. On arriving in the church the *Benedictus* and *Te Deum* were sung, and after customary ceremonies the bishop delivered a short sermon explaining the principles of government.

He then proceeded to the presbytery where he designated six canons, who had previously submitted to him, and likewise two young clerics studying there. Then at four o'clock, he made his way to the abbey. The first gateway was opened to him by a Swiss guard in green uniform. The Tower doorway was deserted and nobody came to the entrance. After waiting some time, Bossuet knocked at the door. The prioress came to the grill and said that the abbey did not depend on any ecclesiastical superior other than the pope; she added that she and her nuns were waiting for the word of the Holy Father's wishes.

Bossuet was obliged to return to the presbytery. That evening he summoned the confessor of the abbey, M. Remond, and the Dominican preacher for Lent, P. Basile, to appear in his presence. He gave orders that the priest was not to confess the nuns and that the Dominican was not to speak in public. Two canons, Nicolas Rassicod and Daniel de La Vallée, who had refused to submit to the bishop, were suspended.

What exactly happened between February 25 and the next

official visit by Bossuet on March 2 of the same year is not known for certain. It seems that the bishop managed to speak to the prioress in the absence of the abbess, and that the prioress gave him to understand that with the exception of some seven or eight indignant nuns, the others would be prepared to submit to him. She, herself, however, could do nothing, for the abbess had written her a hasty letter instructing her not to give way.

Once again Bossuet presented himself at the abbey on Thursday, March 2, and again the Swiss Guard in green livery opened the first gateway, but the main doorway remained closed. Bossuet demanded entrance in accordance with his ordinance of February 23. This time the fiscal procurator of the abbey, M. Cheverry, confronted Bossuet and together with other representatives of the office of the abbey, made a formal protest in the name of the prioress and the nuns.

Bossuet claimed his right of jurisdiction over the abbey in accordance with the decrees of the councils of Trent and Vienna. Backed by the ordinances of De Blois, Lieutenant General Sieur, the representative of the army, who had come with him, and by virtue of the decree that he had brought with him, Bossuet commanded that the door be opened.

As this was not complied with, two workmen were told to force the locks, which they proceeded to do. But before completely breaking the lock, the nuns from within opened the door so as to stop the ruin of their property. The nuns immediately retired through the door of the cloister.

Once inside the abbey, Bossuet walked about until he encountered a nun, and he asked her to take him to the community. He succeeded in assembling some of the nuns in one of the rooms, although not the Chapter House, which was closed. Then he read the decrees of the Council of Trent and the Council of Vienna to the nuns so as to justify his actions.

What chance had the nuns to study the statutes of the Council of Trent? Pope Pius V had abandoned the publication of the Acts, and when they did come out it was in two different versions.[24] Had the nuns read them carefully they would have seen the fallacy of Bossuet's arguments. It is true that at the twenty-fifth session it was decreed that women's religious orders immediately subject to the Apostolic See should be governed by the bishop of the diocese, not by virtue of his office, but as a special delegate of the Apostolic See. This, however, was only to take place if the religious order, after a reminder from the metropolitan bishop, had refused to form itself into an association with another congregation as requested by the Council of Trent, in which case the abbey would come under the superior general of the congregation and not the bishop. But Bossuet never asked the Abbey of Jouarre to join a congregation; while the Abbey of Faremoutier, which sought to join a congregation, was stopped by Bossuet from doing so. The Archbishop of Paris had been officially appointed as papal delegate for the visitation of the Abbey of Jouarre, so that Bossuet had no right to appropriate it to himself. Furthermore, in the case of royal abbeys, the kings' agreement had to be given. But these points were not mentioned by Bossuet in his address to the nuns of Jouarre.

Owing to insufficient knowledge on the part of the nuns, Bossuet's speech won over several of them to his side. The next day, March 3, Bossuet wanted to celebrate Mass in the church of the abbey, but he found it locked. Again he called on the assistance of the lay arm, and the door was forced open. The procurator of the abbey, M. Cheverry, protested again on behalf of the abbey, without effect. After Mass, Bossuet gave Benediction and visited the sacristy. On finding it in good order he retired to the presbytery. In the afternoon Bossuet sent a representative to the abbey, but he was unable to find anyone to whom to speak. Bossuet, undaunted, resorted again to the lay arm, this time by having the grill and the door of the cloister broken. Two portresses came to the door. The bishop became aware of the absurdity of his position. He demanded the keys of the abbey, but the portresses refused. So Bossuet had a chain put on the doorway, and keys fastened to it, and took the key away with him, so contenting himself by symbolically holding the right over the place.

The next day Bossuet once more celebrated Mass with full solemnity, wearing the most magnificent vestments. In the evening he gave the key of the chained doorway to one of the nuns who submitted to him. The canon, Nicolas Rassicord, who earlier had refused to accept Bossuet, now submitted. Subsequently the prioress and six nuns submitted. The abbess left the Abbey of Jouarre and went to Port Royal, where the Abbess of that abbey, the sister of the Archbishop of Paris, gave her a warm welcome.

By various documents that have been preserved we can see that it is certain that the Abbess of Jouarre, Henrietta of Lorraine, was very active in her defense. She wrote several times to the Holy See, but she complained that her letters were intercepted.[25] Pope Alexander VIII, who had shown interest in supporting the abbess, died in March 1692. Shortly afterward Henrietta decided to abdicate her position as abbess and nominated in her place Marguerite de Rohan. Henrietta retired to Port Royal, where she died January 25, 1694.

Marguerite de Rohan was young, only twenty-eight years old. Although she submitted to Bossuet, she would not agree to receive the ceremony of the consecration as abbess from his hands. She waited until after his death ten years later (1707), and the ceremony was performed by her brother, the Cardinal of Strasbourg, in Paris.

THE FRENCH REVOLUTION AND SUPPRESSION OF THE ABBEY OF JOUARRE

The royal Abbey of Jouarre, in the same way as all other religious orders in France at the time of the French Revolution, suffered complete ruin. In 1789, the community consisted of thirty-one choir nuns, twenty-two lay sisters, and many dependent families and farms on their surrounding territories, with most of the people in the employment of the abbey. By decrees of April 14 and 20, 1789, all property had been declared as belonging to the National Assembly. It took effect slowly. On April 30, 1790, the Director of its district arrived at the abbey accompanied by civil officers to list all titles and deeds of its property, furniture, and goods. After this the community was left in peace until 1792, when on September 9 the nuns were told to prepare to evacuate the abbey in twelve days.

Some of the disbanded nuns succeeded in working together, running a girls' school, and gradually reestablished the community. Inspired by the spirit of the liturgy rekindled by Dom

Gueranger O.S.B. the abbey has once more become a flourishing Benedictine Convent; but the sisters sing alone, apart from the parish. The abbess holds no jurisdiction over the town or the people.

THE ABBEY OF FONTEVRAULT

Among the many religious orders that had abbesses with quasi-episcopal jurisdiction in France, the Abbey of Fontevrault is particularly interesting for its connection with the English throne through Eleanor of Aquitaine, Queen of England, and for the three Fontevrault houses in England that are known to have been similarly exempt from the jurisdiction of the bishops.

The Order of Fontevrault was established in the first decade of the twelfth century. It was intended chiefly for the advantage of women attended by the services of priests and brothers in the chivalrous spirit typical of the age. The priests and monks together with the nuns took vows of obedience to the abbess in imitation of the obedience of Jesus to his mother, while the abbess in imitation of Mary served the community devotedly in an administrative capacity.

Fontevrault Abbey is still standing, although it is now a museum. It is situated to the south of Tours and to the north of Poitiers. There were many buildings. The main one, the "Grand Moustier," was for the women; it was joined to the abbey Church of Saint Mary. The monks' house stood separately to the northeast of the abbey and was approached by an alley of elms. It was dedicated to Saint John the Evangelist, who was chosen as patron saint because as the adopted son of Mary he likewise served her in a spirit of obedience. A second women's convent, founded for widows, was dedicated to Mary Magdalene. It was also open to women of low repute wishing to reform their lives. A third convent for nuns was dedicated to Saint Benedict. Besides these, there was a hostel for visitors and a separate house for novices. There was a school for children of noble families. A house, built at a later date, was for the royal princesses of France. There they were received as infants, and there they lived until old enough to return to the court. Like all religious orders, they had a hospital. It was for lepers, and it was dedicated to Saint Lazar.[26]

Robert d'Abrissel, the founder of Fontevrault, was a native of Brittany, where double communities of monks and nuns had flourished, and where it would have been considered quite normal for the abbess to be head over both monks and nuns. It is possible that Robert d'Abrissel took the Abbey of Loc Maria as his model.[27]

Hersende de Champagne, the first prioress, died at an early age, so that it was Petronille de Chemillé who was elected the first abbess and who was installed on October 28, 1115 before a community of five thousand nuns and again as many monks.[28] Robert d'Abrissel, known as the Master, knelt before Abbess Petronille, whom he entitled "Servante des Servantes de Dieu" and made his first vows of obedience to her. The others all followed suit. This was the ceremony that was perpetuated through the centuries until the suppression of the order at the time of the French Revolution.

Pope Calixtus II confirmed the election of the Abbess Petronille by a bull dated October 17, 1119.[29] Earlier in the same year the pope had visited the foundation while on a tour in Poitou, after the Council of Rheims, when he consecrated the Church of Saint Mary in the presence of cardinals, bishops, and many eminent persons. The pope recognized the abbess as head of both men and women members and he acknowledged her right to exemption. It was Petronille who gave the first rule to the order, which was followed in all foundations. The order became enormously popular in France, England, and Spain. In England, houses of Fontevrault were founded at Nuneaton in 1155 and in Westwood in the same year. At Amesbury a community adopted the Fontevrault Rule in the place of the Benedictine one, owing to a deterioration of the earlier foundation. When Pope Alexander III issued a bull extending the privilege of exemption of the mother house from episcopal jurisdiction to all the Fontevrault houses, the ones in England automatically obtained the same rights. However the abbesses of these houses were dependent on the abbess of the mother house, not directly dependent on the Holy See. This continued until the fourteenth century in England because King Edward II in 1317[30] wrote to the Abbess of Fontevrault asking her to appoint his sister Mary, a nun of Amesbury, as visitor to the houses of the order in England instead of sending an alien representative. The king assured the abbess of his sister's capacity to hold this office, for she was known not to deviate from right when undertaking such visitations. So at this time women were appointed to make the visitations of religious houses; at a later date only bishops and cardinals were appointed visitors.

The most famous Fontevrault foundation in Spain was the Abbey of Marie de Vega.[31] After the death of Robert d'Abrissel, the number of Fontevrault nuns was given as five thousand in a letter of Eugenius III, and the number reached nine thousand in 1248 under Pope Innocent IV.

The fundamental spirituality of the order was based on the words of Our Lord on the Cross when he said to Mary: "Mother, here is your son" and to John: "Son, here is your mother." Robert of Abrissel explained the text as meaning that when John took Mary as his own mother it was to serve her with the spirit of obedience of a son.

Petronille de Chemillé governed the abbey with success for thirty-five years. After her death, Matilda, the daughter of Falk V, was elected as second abbess. She came up against the Bishop of Poitiers, who refused to install her unless she took an oath of obedience to him [32] and unless the community should come under his jurisdiction. Suger, the famous Abbot of Saint Denis, came to the assistance of Fontevrault by writing a letter to Pope Eugenius III certifying that he had personally witnessed the conferring of the pivilege of exemption upon Fontevrault. Eugenius, thereupon, sent a bull confirming the right of Fontevrault and insisting that the bishop give episcopal benediction without any conditions.

Nevertheless, trouble arose again when the third abbess was elected. This time the Abbot Pierre of Chelles, Troyes, and Saint Remi interceded for Fontevrault. He wrote a letter to Alexander III complaining that the Bishop of Poitiers was trying to force the abbess elected for Fontevrault to be under his jurisdiction, whereas the abbey had the privilege of direct dependence on the Holy See, and Abbot Pierre asked the pope not to abandon them to others and not to admit any mediator, but to favor them with his protection.[33]

Alexander did as required, and, in fact, he sent them eight bulls confirming their privilege during his pontificate. In a bull addressed to all the bishops and archbishops in whose diocese there were foundations of the Order of Fontevrault, he extended the privileges to all houses of the Order and also denied the bishops the right to excommunicate the nuns or the monks of Fontevrault.[34]

While the order was under the protection likewise of the Plantagenet kings and queens of England, especially Eleanor of Aquitaine, wife of Henry II, the order flourished. Both Henry and Eleanor maintained a great devotion for the foundation of Fontevrault and gave it full protection and many donations; they selected it for their family vault and burial place. Hence the tombs of Henry and Eleanor, Richard Coeur-de-Lion and his queen, Isabel, and the third wife of King John are still to be seen there.

By the end of the thirteenth century and during the fourteenth century the abbey suffered from ruinous wars, famine, and the effects of the Black Death. The plague had a world-wide disastrous result on religious orders in general. The number of nuns at Fontevrault houses dropped from five thousand to five hundred in 1246. In 1296, Boniface VIII limited their number at the abbey to three hundred.[35]

The priors went beyond their rights by selling land without the permission of the abbess. A bull of Alexander IV dated 1259 insisted on the affiliated houses being absolutely dependent on the mother house.[36] The Abbess Blanche d'Harcourt was obliged to give a prison sentence in order to obtain obedience. The monks complained of being subject to the abbess, quite forgetting the spiritual inspiration of the founder. They likewise disliked having to genuflect every time they passed in front of the abbess. The nuns reacted by refusing to kneel in the confessional before their brothers. They asked John XXII for permission to confess their small and secret imperfections to one another rather than expose themselves to the shame of speaking about these things to men. This is a story told by Rabelais,[37] who was fond of expressing himself in a farcical fashion so he may have exaggerated the account.

During the wars nuns had been sent back to their families for protection. When they returned to the abbey they brought with them their personal possessions, which they kept in their individual cells. The superfluous was added to the necessary, and community goods were not shared. In this we can see the confusion of the ideas: the holding of personal goods was right for canonesses but not for nuns of religious orders.

THE REFORM BY ABBESS
MARIE DE BRETAGNE

It was the Abbess Marie de Bretagne, elected in 1457, who undertook the unpopular task of reforming the order. Owing to the resistance on the part of some of the nuns and monks, she retired with a small select group of nuns and monks to the House of La Madeleine d'Orléans. Assisted by a commission named by Sixtus IV, she wrote the new statutes for the order.[38] The main changes were with regard to vows of poverty and to stricter enclosure. Every candidate should be considered without regard to their dowries. Community property was carried to such an extreme that no nun could have her own ink pot, pen, or writing block. Novices among the nuns could not be received before ten years of age, and they could not be professed before fourteen years of age, later changed to sixteen. Men could not enter before fifteen years of age and be professed earlier than eighteen years of age.[39]

There was a change in the formulas used for the vows. Nuns took a vow of enclosure and adherence to the new rule. The clergy were no longer directly dependent on the abbess as before, but via the bishop: *Ego frater N . . . , clericus, diocesis N . . . proponens Ancillis Christi usque ad mortem, cum debitae subjectionis Reverentia, servire. . . .*[40]

This shows a loss of status on the part of the abbess, for before she had been directly responsible for her clergy who made their oaths to her without dependence on a bishop, in the same way as at Jouarre, Conversano, Burgos, and other places.

The monks and nuns of the House of La Madeleine d'Orléans accepted the new statutes in 1475. Three years later two other priories adhered: Fontane-en-France and Chaise-Dieu in Normandy. But the mother house and others refused. In 1476, the pope approved the new statutes. A year later Marie de Bretagne died. It was Renée de Bourbon, called the "Pearl" of Fontevrault, abbess for forty-three years, who completed the reform and put it into effect. She was Abbess of the Sainte Trinité of Caen as well as Fontevrault, and likewise reformed it. The Sainte Trinité of Caen was a women's monastery, which together with the men's monastery at Caen, was founded by William the Conqueror and Queen Matilda. It remained exempt and of independent jurisdiction until the eighteenth century.

The reform of Fontevrault was no easy task. After trying for twelve years without success, Renée retired to Paris and then returned to Fontevrault with solicitors and the military arm to assist her. She built a tower, and she had a grill installed, which was subsequently torn down during the night. Most of the monks and nuns left, so that the abbess remained with only nine professed nuns and five lay sisters. Nuns from earlier reformed houses were invited to fill the place of the nuns who had left. The new community took their vows of enclosure June 13, 1505. The dissident monks were rallied by Parlement, and by military force they were obliged to ask the abbess pardon for their refusal to comply with the new regulations. Pope Clement VII approved these reforms, and they were also ratified by the Grand Council of the king.[41]

The example of Fontevrault was followed by other orders: Chelles, Jouarre, and Sainte-Croix at Poitiers, each introducing their own reforms. It is important to note that these reforms took place before the Council of Trent.

REBELLION OF THE MONKS TO THE VOW OF OBEDIENCE TO THE ABBESS

The monks had become restive ever since the reform had been made by the Abbess Marie de Bretagne. In 1636 the monks obtained a papal brief permitting them to revise their own statutes. They sought to establish rules by which they could evade the jurisdiction of the abbess, and they planned to take over the main building belonging to the nuns. They offered to provide three other houses for the nuns.

The Abbess Jeanne-Baptiste de Bourbon declared the request an abuse. The monks thereupon threatened to leave. So the abbess asked the monks to select a commission of three of their members in order to debate the situation with representatives of the nuns at a meeting over which she presided. As no conclusion was reached, King Louis XIII, the brother of the abbess, intervened.[42] He arranged for the case to be heard in Paris and appointed a commission of nine persons consisting of the Bishop Frémiot of Bourges, the Bishop Cospéan of Lisieux, the Bishop Seguer of Meaux, three members of the king's Council, and three doctors of theology. The abbess was invited by the king to be present.[43]

At the hearing the monks maintained that under the pretext of procuring a reform of the order the position of the monks had been disparaged to the advantage of the nuns. By prohibiting the possession of personal goods the monks were made absolutely dependent on the nuns for their nourishment, dress, and wood for heating. They accused the nuns of being capricious and ungracious, making difficulties over the slightest request, keeping rigidly to the rule of one new habit every two years—forcing the monks to put up with old things—no matter the dilapidated condition of their clothes.[44]

The monks proceeded to the main reason for their rebellion: they considered obedience to the abbess—that is, of men to a woman—against nature and God. The abbess replied that the act of obedience in the Order of Fontevrault was as fundamental as the rule of silence was in the Order of Chartreuse.

The side of the abbess had been defended throughout the lawsuit by Fr. Nicquet S.J., author of the book on the Order of Fontevrault written in the seventeenth century. In his explanation of the abbesses' jurisdiction he referred to the parallel of Deborah, the prophetess and judge of the people of Israel. The same example was brought up by Calvin to justify the right for queens to rule.[45] The idea that nuns, like married women, must be subject to men arose at the time of the Renaissance when the Greco-Roman culture adverse to women was revived. The obedience of clergy and monks to the abbess was considered a worthy ideal in the twelfth and thirteenth centuries; one based on the imitation of Jesus Christ and not degrading to man. But by the sixteenth and seventeenth centuries it was looked upon as being contrary to the nature of man and to the will of God.

The force of an age-long tradition was, nevertheless, allowed to prevail. The council confirmed the authority of the abbess.

The Abbess Jeanne-Baptiste de Bourbon hastened to have the Rule printed in 1642 and distributed it to all the members of the order. In it she was given the title of Chief and General of the Abbey of Fontevrault, directly dependent on the Holy See.

At this time there were 230 nuns and 50 monks at the mother house, with many employed lay people for the hospitals and schools and general service of the abbey. The abbess was responsible for the nomination of the clergy and the payment of their benefices for the forty rectories, chapels, and churches, and for the hundred prioresses dependent on the centralized government of the abbey. The abbess selected the priors herself and gave them the necessary license to preach, to confess, and to serve the women's houses. She had the right to allow confessors to absolve cases reserved usually to bishops. All these powers were likewise held by the abbesses of Las Huelgas, the Cistercian Abbey at Burgos.[46] An Apostolic Visitor was elected every three years by the members of the order in general assembly.[47] The abbess was responsible for both the spiritual and temporal interests of the order.

Owing to the many possessions of the abbey there were constant lawsuits that were held at a court in Saumur. The abbess had a special place built for herself and her nuns when having to attend to this business. It was called the *"logis des Dames de Fontevrault.*[48]

During the *Grande Époque* of France, at the time of Louis XIV, the Abbey of Fontevrault was known for its culture and as an academy of science and literature. The thirty-third abbess, Marie Madeleine Gabrielle de Rochechouart, read the Old Testament in Hebrew, spoke both Italian and Spanish, translated works by Plato and Homer's *Iliad* into French.[49] She corresponded with Racine, Boileau, Gaignière, and the painter Mignard.[50]

The abbess came up against one of the regulations of the Council of Trent, by which it was necessary for nuns wishing to absent themselves from their enclosure to apply to the bishop for permission. Nuns used this law to by-pass the abbess. The bishops, who begrudged the abbesses their independent jurisdiction, easily gave the permission requested by the nuns, although the bishops were in no position to know whether the nun was a responsible person or not. When the Bishop Saint-Fleur of Poitiers brought up a case against the abbess herself, she wrote to Louis XIV saying that as the abbey had had exemption from the bishop for six centuries, she did not consider herself in the wrong for going without his permission. Through correspondence with Madame Maintenon, powerful solicitors were employed to justify her case, and the bishop dropped the lawsuit for fear of an unfavorable sentence.[51]

At the time of the French Revolution the Abbey of Fontevrault capitulated in the same way as other religious houses. The order of evacuation was given on September 30, 1792. The last Abbess of Fontevrault, Julie-Sophie Gilette took refuge with some of the nuns in the environs of Angers. The parish register of the municipal archives of Fontevrault show that the priests were forced to renounce their sacred orders and to get married. Jean Souché, a monk of the abbey, solemnly renounced his priesthood and declared his firm resolve to marry a *"Républicaine laborieuse, douce et vertueuse"* as soon as possible.[52] Julien Moulier likewise solemnly renounced his priesthood, delivered his canonical papers into the hands of the municipality, and pleading illness, requested the right to marry a *"Républicaine compatissante"* to look after him.[53]

Unlike Jouarre, the Order of Fontevrault has not been revived. The history of the order stands witness to the continuation through many centuries of the early Christian tradition in which women were given positions of authority over men and women with approval of the Holy See.

ORDER OF SAINTE–CROIX POITIERS

Canoness Institutes, contrary to religious orders by the very nature of their apostolate connected with that of the deaconess, were naturally dependent on the bishop of the diocese. Only when the abbess herself was a metropolitan episcopa or overseer of a town was she exempt from another diocese. Such was the case of the Abbess Matilda of Quedlinburg.[54] In Gaul, which comprised what today is France and Belgium, there were many Canoness Institutes: at Saint Waudru, Mons, as already mentioned, Nivelles, Ardenne, Malbodio, Demain, Moustier, and others.

One would expect the Order of Sainte-Croix at Poitiers, founded by Saint Radegonde, to be a Canoness Institute. Saint Radegonde had herself ordained deaconess, but she did not make herself head of her order. She established a large hospital that was served by the members of the order. The baptistery of the town in which the order was founded was called the baptistery of the abbey. The service of the baptistery and the service of hospitals was the usual work of deaconesses and hence of canonesses.

As at Saint Waudru, we have evidence of documents regarding the Abbey of Sainte-Croix that were burned because they did not contain evidence to the taste of Dom Fonteneau.[55]

Whatever the Order of Sainte-Croix was at the beginning, it went through several phases: it adopted the Rule of Saint Caesarius of Arles and later that of the Benedictines.

There was a Priory of Saint Radegonde that was in service of the Order of Sainte-Croix and was closely linked with the abbey. There was a considerable amount of friction between the canons and the women's order. In 1072 Pope Alexander II laid down the rights of the abbess over the canons.[56] It is to be noted here that the matter was being regulated from Rome and not from the bishopric of Poitiers. Later bulls of several popes confirmed the duty of the canons to serve the abbey. Furthermore, it was stated that the abbess alone had the right to confer the investiture on the abbot.

In 1165 Pope Alexander III took the abbey officially under the protection of the Holy See and confirmed its right of possession of various domains and of churches under its jurisdiction.[57]

In 1367 the canons sought to take over control and excommunicated the nuns of Sainte-Croix for not having contributed the seven pounds of candle wax and twenty-five sous that the nuns were held to pay. But the excommunication was absolved by higher powers.

Until the beginning of the sixteenth century the members of the Order of Sainte-Croix received prebends—that is, salaries—as was usual for secular canonesses. That they were secular canonesses is likewise proved by the existence of the ten or so residencies called priories that were inhabited and run by women members of the order. Each priory received a certain sum from the abbess according to documents of the second half of the thirteenth century.[58] The Abbess Isabeau de Couhé (1455–1484) initiated a reform of the abbey, and she suppressed a number of the priories in order to augment the funds for the general expenses of the community. The reform followed the lines of the reform of the Order of Fontevrault by Marie de Bretagne, and likewise came up against great opposition from members of the abbey. Finally community life was introduced in the way usual to nuns of religious orders, and the Abbey of Sainte-Croix lost its canonical status.

During the French Revolution the abbey was dissolved as were other orders elsewhere. However, the nuns managed to remain in small groups close to the abbey. Eventually they were able to get together again, and after a period during which a school was run for financial reasons, the Abbey of Sainte-Croix became an entirely contemplative order without the distraction of school work, and it is now a flourishing Benedictine community.

CONCLUSION

It is now possible to observe the general trend of events. The abbesses of both religious orders and of Canoness Institutes held high responsibilities. The abbess of a religious order was an ordained person even though those under her were not so. The abbess of the Canoness Institutes was ordained, and so were some of the members. The abbesses of both religious orders and Canoness Institutes looked after the churches in their large domains. The abbesses of religious orders were exempt from the jurisdiction of a bishop and directly dependent on the Holy See. The abbesses of Canon Institutes would normally be dependent on a bishop, but due to the withdrawal of some of the services of the deaconess-canoness, the two types of communities were confused, and later Canoness Institutes were also taken under the protection directly of the Holy See. The litigations between the bishops and the religious orders made it necessary for the Holy See to take steps to solve the difference of opinion. On the whole, we see that the papacy took the side of the religious orders.

The royal Abbey of Notre-Dame de Jouarre gives us a good example of an exempt religious order from the seventh century. The fact that the earliest documents stating exemption can only be traced to the twelfth century is understandable given the ravages of war and other disasters. The abbeys of Rebais and Faremoutier claimed the same rights from the time of Bishop Faron in the seventh century, and such a claim conforms with the general exemption given by Pope Gregory I to all Benedictine monasteries, later given to other orders.

The fact that the abbesses of Jouarre were the heads of the churches, the clergy, and the people in their "separated" districts was in no way extraordinary. It was in keeping with the usual practice of exempt orders. What is astounding is the terrible change of attitude that took place after so many centuries of a Christian tradition, a tradition in which women's administration had been accepted and enjoyed. It was, after all, a service to the advantage of the Church when by devotion, lands were handed over to the orders in order to be developed for the good of the Church.

It was only after the twelfth century when there was a slow return to Greco-Roman culture reaching its zenith during the Renaissance that the services rendered by abbesses was looked upon as wrong. The example of Bossuet's enforced domination over the Abbey of Jouarre was a flagrant contradiction of the earlier Christian ideal of monastic freedom. The dislike of women having any right to rule shows that the whole idea of what it means to rule had become repaganized. Administration was no longer considered a service but a right of dominion, a right to laud it over another, which was the pagan idea of government and not the Christian one of humble service.

The change of attitude can be seen very clearly also in the

case of the Order of Fontevrault. At the beginning, the obedience of the founder Robert d'Abrissel, of the clergy, and of the monks to the abbess was considered a very lovely and commendable act in imitation of the obedience of Jesus to his mother and of John the Evangelist in service of his adopted mother. It was not until the fifteenth and sixteenth centuries onward that the vow gave rise to indignation on the grounds that it was wrong for a man to make a vow of obedience to a woman.

The litigations in the Order of Sainte-Croix at Poitiers, when the prior did not want to be installed by a woman; the attempt of the canons and clergy of Saint Waudru to turn out the canonesses from their choir stalls in the collegiate Church of Saint Waudru; and the more successful occasions when the clergy did succeed in turning women out of the choir stalls at Milan are examples of the devastating change that took place.

All these things have become hidden history. Nobody hears anything about it. It is hushed up, and the Christian tradition is presented as an all-male right of authority as though it had been so always. Whereas in fact the quasi-episcopal status of abbesses did not come to an end until the time of the French Revolution. And we shall see in the case of Las Huelgas de Burgos the same status continued until 1874.

CHAPTER SEVEN

QUASI-EPISCOPAL ABBESSES IN GERMANY

THE QUEDLINBURG INSTITUTE

THE ABBESSES OF THE QUEDLINBURG INSTITUTE were in control of the whole town, its people, churches, hospitals, clergy, canons and canonesses, and all religious orders. The daughter of Otto I, the Abbess Matilda, was called a *Metropolitana*, and, she held the jurisdiction of a bishop.

The town of Quedlinburg was built by Heinrich I, "the Fowler." He gave the town to his wife Matilda in the same way as Otto I gave the town of Magdeburg to Queen Edith. Adelheid, the sister of Heinrich, was entitled by the historian George Fabricius as *Sacerdos Maxima* of Quedlinburg.[1] Kettner, another historian calls her the "*Oberste Dom-Frau*,"[2] the superior canoness of the cathedral. A *Dom-Herr* is a canon of a cathedral. It has already been established that canonesses did function together with canons in cathedrals, such as at Monza, Italy,[3] and at Saint Waudru's in Mons, Belgium,[4] in the last case until the end of the eighteenth century. Before the building of the Monastery on the Mount overlooking the town of Quedlinburg, the original *coenobio* of the canonesses must have been within the town and close to the cathedral.[5] This would explain the confusion regarding the tomb of Heinrich, which some documents state was at the altar of Saint Peter's in the town, while others say it was in the cloister, which later writers automatically assumed meant outside the town and on the Mount. It can be concluded that at one time the canonesses and canons of Quedlinburg functioned together in the cathedral in the town and that at a later date the monastery was built on the Hill and the canonesses moved out.

Many early papal bulls gave the Quedlinburg Institute a right of exemption. A bull of Pope John XIII (968) gave exemption from the emperor, king, bishop, or any sacred or civil authority.[6] A bull from Pope Sylvester II (999)[7] to Abbess Adelheid II gave a long list of possessions under her jurisdiction. Another bull of Pope Lucius III[8] (1184) confirmed the same.

There is an interesting tombstone in Quedlinburg with an inscription regarding Matilda, daughter of Otto I, in which she is said to be *metropolitana* and abbess of the city and *matricia* of Saxony.[9]

The title *metropolitana* is considered unique by Stengel. But we have seen that the first wife of Otto I, Edith, was head of the city of Magdeburg, and that Adelheid, his second wife, was head of Pavia. Queen Matilda, the wife of Henry I, governed the town of Quedlinburg until 968, and she was, furthermore, head over the abbesses of Winithusen, Nordhausen, Richeberg, and Pölden.[10]

Matilda's brother, Otto II, made it his policy to appoint a *patricius* or a *matricia* for certain regions. He named Ziago as *patricius* of Rome, Boleslaw as *patricius* of Poland, and the Abbess Matilda as *matricia* of Saxony.

The appointment of an abbess to such a position was not unusual, as the abbesses of Quedlinburg normally had a seat and vote in the Imperial Diet, the *"Reichstage zu Regenberg."*[11] In 973, Otto I held an important meeting at Quedlinburg, to which he invited representatives of the Danes, the Bohemians, the Poles, the Russians, the Bulgarians, the Hungarians, the Greeks, and the Italians; and of course the abbess would have taken part. Also abbesses in England were called to parliament during the reign of Edward III,[12] so it was not unusual.

Otto II married the Greek princess Theophanu. Their daughters all became important abbesses: Adelheid II of Quedlinburg was at first Abbess of Nivelles until the death of Matilda; Sophia became Abbess of Gandersheim after the death of Geberga; Ida became Abbess of Saint Mary's Cologne, Hedwig, Abbess of Neuss; Theophanu, Abbess of Nivelles; and Matilda, Abbess of Villach and Diedenkirchen. These monasteries were all institutes of secular canonesses. They struck their own coins, which bore the heads of the abbesses. Otto III was three years old when his father, Otto II, died. The Empress Theophanu and the widow of Otto I, Empress Adelheid, ruled the Empire during Otto III's minority.

Matilda and Adelheid and the later Abbess Sofia of Quedlinburg are all termed *Sacerdos Maxima* by Fabricius, as are many other abbesses of German monasteries.[18] The Abbess Adelheid of Quedlinburg became likewise Abbess of Gandersheim. Pope Sylvester II confirmed her election. Later she visited Pope Benedict at Bamberg. In 1085, Pope Clement VIII held a synod at Quedlinburg, so as Saint Hilda's foundation in England and the royal Abbey of Jouarre, women's monasteries have been chosen as suitable places for holding Church Councils, and there can be no doubt that the abbesses took part.

In 1021, Bishop Arnolphus of Halberstadt reconsecrated the monastery of Mount Sion after the first monastery had been destroyed by fire. It was at this time that he started the custom, which was to last for centuries, of a Palm Sunday procession to the cloister on Mount Sion. Prelates and laity swarmed up the hillside and feasted at the top at the expense of the nuns, who supplied quantities of fish to the crowds. At the beginning of the eleventh century the monastery was still rich and able to offer this quite magnificent spread. But in the thirteenth century the institute was no longer well off, and when one of the abbesses, Abbess Sophia, stopped the procession from coming, she provoked a major litigation between the Bishop of Halberstadt and the monastery.

The election of Abbess Sophia, daughter of the Emperor Frederick II, was recognized by Pope Innocent III, who confirmed also her privileges of exemption. The procession on Palm Sunday was then considered a very important feast both in the East and in the West. Bishop Misnen of Halberstadt considered the refusal of the procession an imposition on his rights, and he excommunicated the abbess and all those dependent on her. Abbess Sophia, on the strength of her exemption, considered she had the right to refuse, and appealed to Rome. Innocent III sent two bulls to the Bishop of Halberstadt upholding the abbess and insisting on her being reinstalled. In the bull dated 1207 he stated very clearly that the bishop had no jurisdiction whatsoever over the abbess either as an ordinary or as a delegate.[14] In the bull of 1210 restating the same thing at still greater length, he mentioned that the abbess had authority over both the clergy and the laity belonging to her.[15] So here we see as at Jouarre that the abbess' jurisdiction over clergy and people was ordinarily accepted.

The members of the Institute at Quedlinburg were clearly called Augustinians in the bull of Innocent III in 1206;[16] that is, they were canonesses, not nuns. But in the same way as at Clerkenwell in England as well as other places, there seems to have been periods when the community adopted the religious rule of nuns. When Otto I built the Monastery on the Mount in 961, he referred to it as *Sanctimoniales Quedlinburgesium*,[17] which encouraged a life of greater solitude and less of service to the people than the group in the town. Nevertheless, in 999, Pope Sylvester called it an *institutione canonica*. In spite of variations, the community retained its initial character of canonesses until the Reformation, when we are told by the historian Fritch that the nuns did not take vows,[18] which was usual in secular Canoness Institutes.

Through all the centuries the popes continued to reaffirm the privileges of the Institute of Quedlinburg until it withdrew from the protection of the Holy See by siding with the Lutherans. In 1539 the Abbess Ann called a consistory, and the decision was taken to adopt the Lutheran rites.[19] The institute continued as a sisterhood, and its renowned school for girls was likewise maintained. In 1697 the Elector of Bradenburg bought the rights over Quedlinburg, now no longer controlled by the institute. The abbesses retained rights of jurisdiction, but there were frequent disputes and finally in 1803, under the Prussian government, the sisterhood was secularized.

From the time of the foundation of the Quedlinburg Institute in the tenth century until the sixteenth century when it became Lutheran, three of the abbesses were given the title *Sacerdos Maxima*. The quesion is whether these three were ordained in the same way as the other abbesses who were not given this title. All abbesses of the institute were exempt and quasi-episcopal. At the Abbey at Gandersheim, which was very closely connected with Quedlinburg, the nun Roswitha was called a *sacerdos*, not *Maxima*. She was in fact not an abbess. The word *Maxima* can be taken to indicate that the person was an abbess. Two documents, one of 1068 and the other of almost two hundred years later, 1241, give a list of witnesses from the Quedlinburg Institute showing that the canonesses held similar posts to that of the canons. They held the offices of *Praeposita*, *Decana*, and *Custos* in the same way as the canons, who are referred to as *Praepositus* (prior) and *Custos*.[20]

We conclude that the canonesses had ordained persons among them. This does not mean that they were ordained to the consecration of the Eucharist; at least, even if they had the right, it would not have been used until they reached fifty or sixty years of age.

THE INSTITUTE OF SAINT MARY'S ÜBERWASSER, MÜNSTER, WESTPHALIA

The interest of the Institute of Saint Mary's, Überwasser lies in its canonical character, in contrast with the Abbey of Jouarre, which was typical of those religious orders that sought retirement from the world. The Canonical Institutes sought to serve the Church in the world.

The clerical state is essential to the Order of Canon Regulars and only accidental to monastic orders, according to the definition of Thomas Aquinas.[21] And Suarez furthermore maintains that both canonesses and canons were of apostolic origin [22] and followed the same rules. Since canonesses, as well as canons, worked for the diocese, they naturally came under the authority of the bishop, and there would not have been any question of the head of the canonesses being a quasi-episcopal abbess with jurisdiction independent of the bishop. On the contrary, we find at

Überwasser that the head of the canonesses, who was also called an abbess, was archdeaconess and representative of the bishop. There was a close relationship between the canons of the Cathedral of Münster and the canonesses of Saint Mary's, Überwasser who were called *consorores*. The women's church was very close to the cathedral, just across a small stream, within a five-minutes-procession distance. It seems to have constituted the same type of double cathedral as in Milan, Pavia, and Brescia, Bergamo and Naples.[23]

The early history of the Institute of Saint Mary's, Überwasser is contained in a document bound at the back of the Gospel Book that belonged to the Institute and that is now at the Münster Staat Archives.[24] Luckily it escaped destruction in the Second World War, when so many other precious manuscripts were lost.

In the surrounding farmlands of Münster, earlier called Mimigernäford, a noblewoman, Regimond, and her daughter, Vrede-rune, near relatives of the Earl Gottfried von Kappenberg, initiated in the eighth century seven churches in different farms on the territory of the family, which can be considered as *"Eigen-kirchen."* A bishopric was established by Friesen Liudger at Mimigernäford in 792. He had studied under Bishop Gregory of Utrecht and Alcuin of York. There is a gap in the documentary information for two hundred years, when the development of further parishes are reported at the time of Bishop Sigfrid (1022–32). Following him, Hermann, who had been a provost of the Cathedral at Cologne (a town where canonesses served in parishes), was made Bishop of Mimigernäford, and it was he and his sister Bertheidis who built the new canonary and Church of Saint Mary's, Überwasser. The Canoness Institute was considered the continuation of the foundation made by Regimond and Vrede-rune.

The canonesses received prebends in the same way as the canons of the cathedral. The prebends consisted, in early centuries, of payment in kind. That is, they were allotted a share of food, carefully calculated according to the service rendered or the position held. This was also the case at the Canoness Institute of Saint Ursula's, Cologne. The canonesses did not have to eat at a community table, nor were they cloistered. They could take leaves of absence for several months at a time, and, after a certain period of service, they could take a whole year's leave. The right for a new candidate to receive a prebend was passed by the vote of the canonesses in chapter. At Waudru, Belgium, we have seen that this was normally the procedure there, although it was often abused by the Counts of Hainaut, who claimed the right to appoint new prebendaries.[25] The abbess of the canoness community of Saint Mary's of *Kapitol* at Cologne once refused to accept the daughter of a certain nobleman on the grounds that their community was not like a religious order to which vocations were presented, but an institute of canoness candidates who were only elected after a period of study and preparation.[26]

The oaths of the abbess taken before being ordained or installed were placed at the back of the Gospel Book mentioned, as well as the oaths of the priests to the abbess. The abbess promised to observe the customs of the church, not to alienate any property of the community without the consent of the members, and to faithfully administer the prebends according to custom. The consensus of the members was necessary for any official document or for the giving of prebends to persons not belonging to the institute. A list of the tithes due were preserved also in the Gospel Book.

The priests promised to be obedient, faithful, and subject to the abbess and to her successors and to all the members of the convent and the Church of Saint Mary's, Überwasser. They promised to rule the parish rightly and to resist persecutors and not to use the benefices for other purposes than for the good of the Church.[27]

FIRST REFORM

The Institute of Saint Mary's, Überwasser remained a secular canoness community until 1460, in spite of the attempts made to reform the canonesses and to bring them in line with the ordinary Benedictine religious communities. The first such attempt was in 1130.[28] The Abbess Geberga von Kappenberg was persuaded by Bishop Egbert (1127–32), to bring about the reform of the institute and to introduce strict enclosure and community living.

However, as soon as the bishop died, the institute returned to its former customs, and the abbess retired to Quedlinburg to remain there until her death in 1137. Meanwhile, Pope Urban IV recognized Saint Mary's, Überwasser way of life in a bull dated 1263, and it was again confirmed by Pope Martin V.

The Church and house of the Institute of Saint Mary's was dedicated on Christmas Day, 1040, in the presence of King Heinrich III and his queen, who bestowed further gifts on the foundation. Bertheidis was called the "Spiritual Mother": *Prima domna et matre nostra spirituale.* The early abbesses were not only superiors and leaders of the canonesses, but they were also archdeaconesses for the diocese and they represented the bishop.[29] They were archdeaconesses too for other parishes—Nienberge, Holthausen, and Neede. The canonesses are given the name *consorores* of the canons of the cathedral. At the death of an abbess, all bells of the churches of Münster were tolled, and the canons of the cathedral processed in a group from the cathedral to the Church of Saint Mary's, Überwasser, where they chanted the vigil of the dead together with the canonesses. After the Requiem Mass and the burial service, the canons again processed back as a group to the cathedral. This custom is known to have existed from 1100 and to have continued until the end of the sixteenth century.[30] It shows the close connection between the canonesses and the canons, and although the canonesses had their own *Eigenkirche* and their own priests whose prebend was given by the abbess and who took oaths of fidelity in the hands of the abbess, the institute was never independent of the bishop or directly dependent on the Holy See like the abbesses of nuns orders. The abbesses of the canonesses were nearer to being bishop coadjutors, rather than holding an independent jurisdiction.

SECOND REFORM

A second reform was attempted in 1483. A commission of the cathedral chapter of Münster elected a nun from the reformed Benedictine Convent of Agidii, Hilburgis von Norrendyn, to be abbess. She was chosen over the head of the canonesses. She was installed against their will on June 24, 1482. But owing to the resistance of the community, she retired again to her former house. But Bishop Heinrich von Schwarzenberg insisted on her being reinstalled with greater pomp even than before and in the presence of eminent people. This time she was accompanied by three other nuns from the reformed Benedictine Convent of Agidii. New laws were drawn up to make the canonesses conform with the Benedictine nun's type of life. Members who did not want to conform to the new rules were given a year in which to make up their minds, and if they chose to retire, the payment of a pension would be allowed them.[31]

The new rule was approved by the Holy See. Several canonesses left and went to live in their own homes. But once again, on the death of the abbess, the community immediately called a meeting of the chapter and chose an abbess in favor of the old rule. A schism in the community was caused by the three nuns from Agidii, and they elected another abbess from among themselves, Sophia Dobbers, and demanded that again those not wishing to accept her should leave and that the pension would be provided as before. The new rule having been approved by the Holy See, the minority of the three nuns succeeded in winning the case against the majority. But there was a further crisis due to insufficient money to pay the pensions. Finding themselves without sustenance, some old canonesses returned to the community.

Meanwhile, in 1493 and 1495, two bulls of Pope Alexander IV recognized the Canoness Institutes of nearby Nottuln and Frechenhorst, permitting the age-long rule for canonesses to be retained. Evidently, they had been approached by their bishops in the same way as the Canoness Institute of Überwasser, requesting them to conform to the Benedictine rule for nuns. But Nottuln and Frechenhorst succeeded in obtaining protection from the Holy See. Saint Mary's of Überwasser was the only reformed community at this time, and it, no doubt due to the example of their sister Canoness Institutes, little by little returned to its former practice.

THIRD REFORM

Another hundred and fifty years passed, and once again the Institute of Saint Mary's, Überwasser was requested to reform and adopt the Benedictine Rule for nuns in its entirety (December 16, 1617).[32] This time the reform was final. In 1617 there were forty choir nuns and forty-three lay sisters. By 1763, after the disasters of the Thirty Years' War and the Seven Years' War, there were only seven choir sisters left. The abbess, seeking to obtain more vocations, got permission from the pope in 1758 to take candidates from non-noble families, which until then had not been possible. But, meanwhile, the Jesuits who had settled in Münster and had founded a philosophical and theological seminary there, were in need of land for a university. Pope Clement XIV suppressed the Institute of Saint Mary's, Überwasser on May 18, 1773, because of its lack of vocations. The school of the institute, which had continued from the beginning through all the adverse years and had maintained a high standard of tuition for girls, was now secularized to the distress of the families of Münster.

CONCLUSION

The secular Canoness Institutes of Germany give us an example of the early Christian system by which women served the Church as deaconesses living together but without strict rules. Meals were not taken in a community hall, members could travel about and absent themselves for several months. Vows of chastity were not taken. Members could leave to get married without causing scandal. When they did so, however, they could no longer receive the prebend; that is, the salary that for a long time was given in certain quantities of food and drink. There was no question of the canonesses separating themselves from the world as was the case of nuns in religious orders. The usual rule was that of Saint Augustine, which was written for canonesses. When at first the Benedictine Rule was practiced together with the rule of Saint Columbanus or Saint Augustine, it seems to have been adapted to the canoness way of life. Later it was applied strictly according to the life of nuns and caused much friction.

The work of the canonesses consisted in the celebration of Divine Office; Matins was the vigil of the Eucharistic service and Laudes the thanksgiving. It was the part of the Church service that did not entail touching the Blessed Sacrament, thought impossible for women during their monthly periods. The canonesses at first celebrated the Divine Office together with the canons in cathedrals; later the women were moved out to a second cathedral or to their private chapels.

Canonesses specialized in teaching. Many schools for girls in Germany became very famous, as was the case in Quedlinburg and in Überwasser. They also ran hospitals, which had developed from the hospices for pilgrims.

Three of the abbesses of Quedlinburg were given the title of *Sacerdos Maxima*, and one of them, Abbess Matilda, was referred to as *Metropolitana*. They exercised the jurisdiction of bishops. This was also true of all the abbesses of Quedlinburg, since the whole order was exempt. It cannot be established at present whether the title *Sacerdos Maxima* gave the abbesses a form of ordination above the others who were not mentioned as being *Sacerdos Maxima*. It can be proved by the rites for the ordination of abbesses in early times as seen in the Wisigothic Sacramentary that abbesses were ordained persons. This does not necessarily mean that they consecrated the Eucharist, and we presume that they would have withheld from doing so until they reached fifty to sixty years of age.

The abbesses of Saint Mary's, Überwasser were not exempt from the jurisdiction of the bishops of Münster. But they held very high positions as archdeaconesses by which they seem to have been like auxiliary bishops, representing the bishop in several towns. The whole community remained in close relationship as *consorores* of the canons of the cathedral. The repeated attempts to reform the Canoness Institute by imposing the Benedictine Rule fully with strict enclosure caused the break-up of the Institute.

CHAPTER EIGHT

QUASI-EPISCOPAL ABBESSES IN ITALY

SAINT BENEDICT'S CONVERSANO

IT WAS IN THE YEAR 1266 that a community of Cistercian nuns arrived in Brindisi as refugees from the Convent of Saint Maria de Verga, Montone, Rumania. The Abbess Dameta Palaeologus was of the imperial family of Constantinople. By ordinance of Pope Clement IV, she was given the monastery and territory of Saint Benedict in Conversano, Apulia. From the very beginning the abbess and the community were established as exempt by papal decree so that they did not come under the jurisdiction of the Bishop of Conversano, but were directly dependent on the Holy See. The Abbess Dameta, as also the abbesses that followed her, had therefore a quasi-episcopal jurisdiction. At the ceremony of the installation of the abbesses they were invested with the clothing and insignia proper to their status, which included the reception of the miter.

Some historians have looked on the powers of the abbesses of Saint Benedict of Conversano as the "usurped" power of the earlier abbots who had left the monastery and whose territories the abbesses had inherited. This shows prejudice and ignorance of the period because the right of exemption was then quite commonly given to women's as well as men's communities. Information has already been given regarding the exempt orders in France and Germany. Exempt orders in Italy were just as usual; had Abbess Dameta been put in possession of the Benedictine nunnery at Brindisi [1] instead of the men's Benedictine monastery at Conversano, she would have inherited far greater possessions and have enjoyed the rights of jurisdiction over some thirty-six parishes and villages instead of the single church and village of Castellana that belonged to Saint Benedict's of Conversano.

Apulia is the district that extends along the east coast of Italy. It had had a tumultuous history, for it was tossed to and fro between Greeks and Latins in pre-Christian and Christian eras. For a time it was under the Byzantine Empire, then it became overrun by the Goths who ruined the cities. While the Lombards and Byzantines fought among themselves, Apulia fell victim to a third party in 840—the Saracens. Otto I and Otto II defended the country against the Saracens, at which time both Bari and Brindisi became places of hospice for crusaders on their way to Jerusalem. The eleventh century was a period of prosperity; cathedrals and churches were built. In 1266 Apulia came under the government of the Angevin family with Charles I as king, whose court was at Naples.

The reason why the monks had deserted the Monastery of Saint Benedict's, some time between 1258 and 1266, is not known for certain. It is supposed that it was due to the community having sided with the excommunicated Emperor Nicolas, who had opposed Charles I and the Holy See. The earlier Benedictine monastery is believed to have been founded in the seventh century, subsequently restored by Godfrey the Norman. It became a royal and imperial monastery at the time of Frederick II. By the bulls of the popes Leo II, Paschal III, and Alexander IV, the abbots were recognized as having the status of *Praelatura Nullius*, that is, with quasi-episcopal jurisdiction. [2]

Most documents sustain the story that the Cistercian nun's community was a refugee group thrust out of their native country by a persecuting government. But the author Francesco Muciaccia, [3] followed by the contemporary writer Giovanni Mongelli. [4] point out that it was unlikely that the nuns were expelled by their government, which at that time was ruled by a relative of the Abbess Dameta, Michael Palaeologus, who then was emperor. Muciaccia suggests that the reason for the nun's flight was more likely due to the fear of Islam, for other Cistercians also left the east at this time. Muciaccia thinks that the Abbess Dameta had written to Pope Clement XIII before leaving. Mongelli even considers that the community may have been invited by the pope to fill the vacated Monastery of Saint Benedict's, Conversano. In any case, on the arrival of the community in Italy, the pope took immediate action. He commissioned Cardinal Rudulfo, the Papal Legate, to King Charles I of Anjou, to introduce the abbess and her community into the monastery at Conversano. Cardinal Rudulfo wrote to Bishop Bartolomeo Polignano, to whom the monks of Saint Benedict had left the care of the administration of the monastery. The cardinal informed the bishop that it was by order of the pope that the monastery should be given to the Abbess Dameta and her community.[5]

The documents relating to these transactions are preserved for us today in the cathedral archives of Conversano. Bishop Bartolomeo showed the letter he had received from the cardinal legate to the civil authorities of Conversano, not, it seems, to the Bishop of Conversano as the monastery did not come under his jurisdiction. The clergy and people of Castellana—a village ten miles away belonging to the monastery—were invited to come to the ceremony of the installation of the abbess and to make their oaths of fidelity to her in the usual manner.[6]

So here, as at Jouarre and at Quedlinburg, the abbess had jurisdiction over the clergy and the people in her territories.

The documents regarding the possession of the monastery and territory of the Benedictine monks in the bulls of 1172 and 1248, which gave authorization to its exemption, were transcribed by request of Abbess Dameta into a single document with three Greek copies, that is, in her own language. The abbess was careful to obtain all early deeds and warrants; besides the ecclesiastical credentials she requested civil recognition from King Charles I. Furthermore, she wrote to Cardinal Rudolfo to ask for the restoration of lands that had been taken away from the monastery by Frederick II.

This careful preservation of documents was to be important as testimony to the rights of the abbey during the period of long litigations that subsequently took place with the bishops of Conversano.

The Monastery of Saint Benedict, still standing today, is a fortresslike construction with high protective walls. It borders close to the back of the Cathedral of Conversano on the north side, while to the south a plain stretches far into the distance. Conversano is a preserved medieval village, situated on a steep incline, with narrow lanes paved with irregular stone slabs, making the descent a perilous undertaking. The richly decorated baroque church of the monastery contrasts strangely with the severe wood-panelled wall and simple choir stalls of the private chapel of the nuns situated on the balcony above the altar of the church. In the chapel, now unused, there lingers still the atmosphere of Cistercian spiritual austerity.

The Abbess Dameta died in 1270, and Isabella, another nun from Rumania, was elected abbess. Her election was confirmed in a letter by Abbot Dolfino, who had been appointed visitor to the community by the General Chapter of the Cistercian Order. He specifically stated the right of the abbess to spiritual and temporal jurisdiction according to the statutes of the Cistercian Order.[7] The same right to spiritual and temporal jurisdiction was given to the Cistercian Abbey of Las Huelgas de Burgos in Spain.[8]

FIRST LITIGATION A.D. 1272

The first litigation between the Monastery of Saint Benedict and a bishop of Conversano occurred in 1272, when the bishop ordained two clerics dependent on the Monastery of Saint Benedict without requesting the customary consent of the abbess. The Abbess Isabella reported the matter to the Holy See. The case was judged by the Archbishop Enrico of Taranto in favor of the abbess, and Pope Gregory X confirmed the right of the abbess over her own clerics.[9]

There was some trouble in 1287 regarding the right of the monastery over the Church of Saint Nicolas in Portu Aspero. The abbess was confirmed likewise in her rights.[10]

FURTHER LITIGATIONS

It was only in the sixteenth century that an antifeminist attitude arose with regard to the jurisdiction of abbesses and that it became a subject of debate, whereas before it had not been questioned. Some clerics belonging to the monastery sought to evade the jurisdiction of the abbess by taking the habit of the Franciscan Tertiaries. The matter was again submitted to the Holy See. Pope Pius V insisted on the submission of the clerics to the authority of the abbess and confirmed her spiritual jurisdiction.[11]

In 1630 the Bishop Vincenzo Martinelli of Conversano sought to interfere in the election of the monastery. He believed he had the right to do so based on the bull *inscrutabili* issued by Pope Gregory XV, in which it was stated that bishops should undertake to supervise the quality of the confessors and preachers in religious orders. But Pope Gregory XV issued a second decree modifying the decree of *inscrutabili*, permitting customs of long standing to prevail and so diminishing the right of bishops to interfere. The exemption of the Abbey of Saint Benedict was reaffirmed on February 28, 1630 by the Sacred Congregation of Religious at Rome.

About thirty years later, in 1659, Giuseppe Palermo, Bishop[12] of Conversano, again attempted to interfere in the affairs of the Cistercians, but the Sacred Congregation reconfirmed the rights in favor of the abbess as established in 1630. Bishop Palermo then attacked the authenticity of the Cistercian's exemption and demanded to see the documents. He meanwhile insisted that the nuns should submit themselves to the obedience of the bishop. His attempted take-over was a forerunner to Bossuet's more successful seizure of power over the Abbey of Jouarre. At Conversano there was no loophole for the bishop to establish his claim because the first abbesses had been so vigilant in obtaining and in preserving their documents. Their rights had been authentically established, and no documents had been lost as at Jouarre. The abbesses proved their case, and the decision of the Rota at Rome was made in their favor with a bull dated 1693.

Now, as at the Abbey of Fontevrault, the clergy of Castellana became restive in the new-found complaint that it was wrong for men to be subject to women. This idea had not existed before the Renaissance and the Reformation.

The clergy of Castellana appeared for the first time in Rome in 1705 and put a series of questions to the Sacred Congregation. They asked whether an abbess had the right to elect as her vicar a priest from outside her own territories. (Presumably the abbess having found opposition among the clergy in Castellana had chosen a priest not belonging to Castellana to act as vicar for her.) The clergy further questioned whether, on the election of a new abbess, they were obliged to pay her homage. They also questioned who had the right to appoint a confessor. To all three questions Rome gave the right to the abbesses as a tradition of long standing. However, in the case of homage being paid to a newly elected abbess, a concession was made, and the clergy were per-mitted to make a bow instead of a genuflection as was done pre-viously when acknowledging the abbess. The confessor was to be appointed by the abbess's personally chosen vicar. So we see here a slow whittling away of the jurisdiction of the abbess.

LITIGATIONS WITH THE BISHOPS
OF CONVERSANO 1748–1810

Once again, in 1748, the Bishop Filippo del Prete of Conver-sano sought to have the right of visitation of the Monastery of Saint Benedict's and to make the congregation subject to his juris-diction.[13] The solicitor for the nuns, Michele Tarsia, was very much in their favor and wrote a book in their defense. But on the death of Bishop Filippo del Prete, when Michele Tarsia was him-self elected Bishop of Conversano, he completely revoked his own arguments and turned against the nuns. Disgusted, the commmu-nity took their stand as a royal monastery and declared their pos-sessions subject to the patronage of the king. In consequence, the dispute was brought before the Royal Law Courts of Saint Clare at Naples and was not taken to the Curia in Rome.

The decision was again given in favor of the monastery, and in-deed it was declared the most splendid jewel of the Kingdom of Naples [14] by those who had made the visitation and gave witness in the court. The monastery was declared in excellent order and in keeping with the Cistercian Rule. The document is dated July 7, 1760.

But the rebellious spirit of the French Revolution was already pervading all Europe. On September 4, 1773, the Canonical Chapter of Castellana made a protest to the Holy See regarding the homage to be paid to the abbess and the tributes and tithes they had to give her. The protest was by no means unanimous; only thirty-eight out of seventy priests attended the chapter, and of these three left before the formula of the protest was drawn up. A further fourteen priests refused to sign. Only eighteen, therefor, out of seventy actually were in favor of the protest. It was a vocal minority that made itself heard quite out of proportion to its numbers. In fact, on the election of the new abbess, two delegates of the canons were sent immediately to do homage at the time of the installation. As to the tithes due to be paid by the canons to the abbess, the case was once more brought before the Royal Law Court, and once again the decision was taken in favor of the abbess.[15]

It was finally the invasion of Italy by the Napoleonic forces that brought the whole system of exemption to an end. Joseph, the brother of Napoleon, was made King of Naples, followed by Joachim Murat. The Kingdom of Naples included the district of Apulia and, therefore, Conversano. There, as in other places, religious orders were either suppressed or put under pro-Napoleonic bishops, so making it possible for Napoleon to keep full control. The prioress of Saint Benedict, Conversano, then governing in the place of the abbess whose election was due, was informed indirectly that the monastery was to be put under the Bishop of Conversano. This was in 1809, just at the time when Pope Pius VII had been taken prisoner. There was neither a pope nor a king to protect the monastery. Nevertheless, as a last desperate attempt to bring King Joachim Murat to their side, the prioress sent a letter to him. The following is a summary of the contents.[16]

The letter acknowledged the decree by which the Bishop of Conversano was to take the Monastery of Saint Benedict into his diocese and so abolish its independent episcopal jurisdiction, although without having received any direct information. The prioress and nuns declared their acceptance of the order with a spirit of resignation, but added at the same time that they considered it their duty to disclose to the king the ancient customs on which their right of exemption depended.

The prioress insisted that it was only by prejudice and ignorance that it was considered an abuse for women to hold a place in the Church hierarchy and to have quasi-episcopal jurisdiction. There was no question of women being ordained priests, but that from apostolic times deaconesses formed an order in the administration of the Church into which women were formally initiated by the laying on of hands. Abbesses and congregations of the monastic system, in both the Latin and Greek churches, were given exemption and a right of jurisdiction over their own "separated territories." It was usual for royal and imperial foundations to have this right—particularly Benedictines and other derivated orders. It was a commonly accepted arrangement; abbots and abbesses normally acquired a rank of honor in the hierarchy.

Van Espen (a well-known canonist), was quoted with regard to the privileges granted by Pope Honorius III in 1224 to the Abbess of Fontevrault, in which she was permitted to nominate confessors and preachers and given the right to absolve cases of excommunication—as indeed was likewise granted to many another abbess in Germany, Belgium, Gaul, and Spain—charging the abbess with the maternal care of the flock of Our Lord.

Van Espen is again quoted from his chapter on canonesses, in which he mentioned the high honor granted them in processions, for they walked in front of the clergy and carried the pastoral cross. Reference was made to the Cistercian women's monastery in Burgos, whose power to hear confession and to read the Gospel and to preach in public was taken away by Pope Innocent III, but not their quasi-episcopal jurisdiction, which would have been likewise retracted had it been considered wrong.

The prioress continued to point out that privileges were granted by kings and pontiffs to men and women superiors of abbeys. She insisted that there were hundreds of proofs to establish the right of Saint Benedict's of Conversano to the title of *Praelatura nullius* granted to the monastery.

After a summary of the history of the monastery and the account of the many papal bulls in its favor, which have already been discussed in the foregoing pages, the prioress concluded by asking the king to consider these historical facts. She assured him that if he would do so, he would realize that it had never been unbecoming nor a monstrous thing (as Murat is reported to have said) for an abbess to have been invested with quasi-episcopal jurisdiction, since from apostolic times women have ranked in the hierarchical order and have been considered worthy of an ecclesiastical ministry, all the more so when an abbess. Abbesses have had places in councils ranking above the clergy; at one time they held the right to confess and to preach; they have had the right to suspend clergy subject to them when necessary and to confer offices and benefices; in short, they have been considered prelates of first rank.

The prioress requested the king to restore their former rights to them. The prioress received no answer. It is known that Murat, no profeminist, had referred to them as the "Monstrosity of Apulia" so showing his complete ignorance of the many other exempt Apulian women's monasteries that had once populated that district. The Bishop Romolo Valentibus of Conversano in 1810 must have been a pro-Napoleonic bishop in order to have maintained his place. He had no hesitation in taking the monastery into his diocese, which was to his advantage. Actually, the monastery was lucky not to have been completely dispersed as many other religious houses had been. For example, the Benedictine Convent at Brindisi was turned into a military barracks.[17]

The bull de ulteriori dated May 30, 1809, confirmed the incorporation of Saint Benedict, Conversano, within the diocese. It was signed by Pius VII during his imprisonment in France, which lasted from 1809 to 1814. The bull is not published in the Bullarium Romanorum; there is a note mentioning that at this time no temporal or spiritual power was exercised by the papacy so that the bull cannot be considered a true judgment of the pope.

After the fall of Napoleon, the restored monarchies were not able to reestablish conditions in Italy as the Spanish monarchy was able to do in Burgos. Italy remained in great political disorder, with distrust between the different states. The Risorgimento, a movement to unite Italy, was anticlerical, so that religious orders again suffered destruction.

In 1862 a commission was set up to make an inventory of all the property and goods of the monastery. Everything was appropriated by the government. By an act of 1866 all corporations and religious orders were suppressed. However, some orders managed to evade the law by claiming an international status. According to the book by S. Simone, the Monastery of Saint Benedict had come to an end at the time he was writing in 1885. But some nuns must have managed to stay on, because Msgr. Galli of Conversano, an octogenarian interviewed by me in 1966, said he remembered the nuns in the early twentieth century. Sisters of another order were introduced alongside the Cistercian nuns to run a school for the village, which is still in existence. The last members of the Cistercians died, and the only relics that remain are the miter and gloves once worn by the abbesses, which are kept intact in the chapel.

OTHER WOMEN'S COMMUNITIES IN ITALY GIVEN THE STATUS OF NULLIUS DIOCESIS

To evaluate the history of Saint Benedict's, Conversano, it is helpful to look at the accounts of some of the other women's orders in Apulia, more especially of the Benedictines. The Cistercians had a stronger position due to their inclusion in the General Chapter of the Order and its unity with other men's and women's Cistercian communities. The Benedictine communities were more isolated and were not united into a congregation with other monasteries at the time of their foundation. But, as we have seen, Benedictines were the first to receive the right of exemption from episcopal jurisdiction from the time of Gregory I.

The women's Benedictine community at Brindisi has already been mentioned as having had independent jurisdiction and having possessed far larger territories than the Cistercians at Conversano, with some thirty-six parishes under the control of the abbess, who appointed the clergy and conferred the benefices.[18] It was founded by Godfrey the Norman and his wife Sichelgaita. The city of Brindisi had been ruined by many wars. Godfrey and Sichelgaita reconstructed the whole town, and at the same time they founded the women's convent called Santa Maria Veterana because it was built on the ruins of the old city in 1090. Later the convent became known as the *Monache Neri*, the black nuns, in contrast to the white nuns of the Premonstratations. From the beginning, the exemption from the jurisdiction of the bishops was requested from the Holy See, and we know by the bull of Gregory IX that this was granted by Paschal II (1099–1118) and agreed to also by the Bishop Godino of Brindisi in 1094. But after the death of Bishop Godino in 1122, the next bishop, Bailardo, was not in favor of the independence of the convent, and he suggested to Honorius II that it should be included under his jurisdiction. The Countess Sichelgaita, by then a widow, insisted on the independence of the community conferred on it by the bull of Paschal II. A commission of bishops and abbots of nearby monasteries was set up to judge the case, and it included Pietro of Otranto, the cardinal deacon legate of the Holy See. The others present were Bishop Formoso of Lecce, Abbot Ambrosio of Saint Stephen's Monopoli, the Prior Arno of the Holy Sepulchre of Brindisi, and Adelhardo, the prior of the hospitals of all the states. Judgment was given in favor of the nuns, and Archbishop Bailardo was given in compensation the Church of Saint Basil of Monopoli. To prevent the question from rising again, another document was drawn up naming all the privileges already given to Santa Maria Veterana, including the many churches dependent on the order. This was signed by all present at the meeting, and the document was duly preserved in the nuns' convent.

In spite of these precautions, the independence of the convent was again disturbed some sixty years later, in 1190, by Archbishop Pietro, who sought to exercise his jurisdiction over the churches belonging to the convent. As the clergy of the churches did not obey him, he disqualified them. Again the Holy See was requested to judge the case, and again the right of jurisdiction was given to the nuns. The archbishop was asked to leave the community undisturbed in its rightful liberties and to withdraw the disqualification of the clergy belonging to it.

In 1233 the bull of Gregory IX confirmed all the churches, property, and privileges of the Abbess Audisia and the nuns of Santa Maria of Brindisi. He based the bull on those of his predecessors Paschal II, Calixtus II, Honorius II, Alexander III, and

Celestine II. He listed all the churches, which constituted a formidable number, and further added the interesting fact that both the Greek and Latin rites could be used.[19]

In 1245 a Benedictine nun, Flamenga from Brindisi, was made abbess of the Convent of Saint John the Evangelist in Lecce, a little further south. The fact that she was chosen from the Benedictine Convent in Brindisi shows that the convent was then in very good repute. The convent in Lecce had been founded by the son of Godfrey the Norman, who had also founded the convent in Brindisi; Agnes, Accardo's sister, was made abbess in 1133 and confirmed by the anti-Pope Anacletus II, signed during his visit to Apulia, while at Oria in March 1134. The bull enjoined the *Praelatura Nullius* accepted by Bishop Gualtiero of Lecce. Alexander III confirmed the privileges again in 1178, taking the monastery under the direct dependence of the Holy See. Likewise the Empress Constanza recognized all the former possessions made to the convent.

All this happened before the Greek community of the Cistercian nuns arrived in Conversano, and it is obvious that in spite of some differences with bishops, the independence of the religious orders was considered normal and right by the abbots, the bishops, and the papal legates. It was also considered right for the churches in the territories of the communities on which they were dependent to be likewise independent of the bishop.

In 1455 Bishop Antonio Riccio caused a lot of trouble to the Benedictine women's community at Lecce because the abbess refused him the right of visitation on the grounds that the abbey was exempt.[20] Bishop Riccio forced his entrance by battering down the doorway, so giving precedence to the same feat performed by Bossuet two hundred years later at Jouarre. The sisters appealed to Rome. Sixtus IV arranged for the case to be heard by Bishop Nardo, Bishop Aquino, and Bishop Castro. They evidently decided the case against Bishop Riccio, for the abbey retained its privileges, and these were confirmed by later popes: by a bull of Clement VII in 1530 and by Paul III in 1543. At the death of Bishop Riccio a very satirical entry was made in the Lecce register stating that he died November 24, 1483, after having held the bishopric for thirty years, during which time he had contributed no other benefit than three doors in wood (!) and a palm tree. It can be taken that the bishop was obliged to repair the doorways he knocked down. This entry shows that the general opinion was against him and in favor of the nuns.

At the beginning of the eighteenth century a move was taken against the independence of religious orders in general and against women's religious orders in particular. In 1713 Bishop Bisanzio of Ostuni took legal proceedings against the Benedictine women's abbey in Ostuni and also against the one in Brindisi. The bishop was called to Rome by the Sacred Congregation; but this time the verdict was given against the nuns, and both communities lost their right of independent jurisdiction. On June 14, 1774, Bishop Antonio Serzale of Brindisi made a public entry into the Church of Saint Maria degli Angeli on the strength of the decree of Benedict XIV issued on October 20, 1773. The bishop took it upon himself on October 9, 1746, to abolish the title that the sisters had always had as *custodians* of the churches. This is the same title held between the eleventh and thirteenth centuries by the Canonesses of Quedlinburg—*custos*—when signing documents.[21] The title was likewise held by nuns in the community of Etheldreda in Ely. Schäfer gives information of yet other communities that held this title.[22] This is an example of how little by little the status of women's service to the Church was diminished.

In 1810, by order of Napoleon, bishops were elected and told to take their sees without canonical investiture. When Pope Pius VII protested, he was taken prisoner and kept in Fontainebleau. Archbishop de Leo, who had been given the task of visiting the houses of the *Benedettini Neri* in the diocese of Lecce and Bari at the time of King Ferdinand, was given the injunction by Murat to visit the women's communities at Ostuni and Oria, which he undertook in 1813. By this time all religious orders were under the diocesan rule with bishops of Napoleon's choosing. By the Guide Book of Brindisi, written in 1890, we learn that the Convent of Saint Benedict was suppressed and was converted into a military barracks.

So, the taking away of quasi-episcopal jurisdiction was a general movement all over Italy and France. It was not particular to Conversano. Murat's abolition of the right was the act of a nonbeliever; he couldn't care less whether there had existed a long tradition in the Church or not. But it had been a truly Christian tradition, and one maintained through many centuries, sustained by papal approval. At one time it was enjoyed and desired by all the people. Today it is hidden history—hardly believed and not understood.

CONCLUSION

The continuous litigations of the Monastery of Saint Benedict with the bishops of Conversano that were settled over and over again in favor of the abbesses show how completely the jurisdiction of the quasi-episcopal abbess was accepted as a normal procedure. The indignation of the nuns when deprived of their age-long prerogatives is likewise a witness to the system having been regarded as a fundamental Christian tradition. The many papal bulls confirming the right of exemption and of spiritual and temporal jurisdiction testify that in the Roman Catholic Church women were given positions of authority through many centuries. This status is now refused to them.

The return to the Greco-Roman depreciatory attitude toward women at the time of the Renaissance had the effect at the Council of Trent of a withdrawal of quasi-episcopal jurisdiction from the women's orders. The suppression of the religious orders during the French Revolution brought the system to an end with the exception of orders in Spain. The partial rehabilitation of religious orders under the rulings of Napoleon's *Concordat* with Rome did not reinstate the exempt abbeys, since all orders came under pro-Napoleonic bishops.

Nevertheless, it remains a fact that in the course of history women have held administrative positions in the Church. To hide these facts is to falsify the true Christian tradition.

CHAPTER NINE

QUASI-EPISCOPAL ABBESSES IN SPAIN

LAS HUELGAS DE BURGOS [1]

BURGOS WAS THE CAPITAL of Old Castile, situated in the northwest of Spain, on the route from France to Compostella, frequented by many pilgrims to the famous shrine of Saint James. It was outside the walls of Burgos and across the river that Alphonse VIII and his wife Queen Leonora of England founded the Abbey of Las Huelgas, with the Hospital "del Rey" for the poor and the sick pilgrims. The abbey was built chiefly by the initiative of Leonora, while the hospital was mainly the undertaking of the king, hence the name of the hospital—"del Rey." In all documents, however, the names of both the king and the queen are included, often also with the names of their children.

Las Huelgas de Burgos was founded as a Cistercian community, and although it was by no means the first, it soon became the "*Matriz*," the chief of all the other Cistercian women's monasteries by the express wish of the king and queen. In fact it became the head at one time of all women's religious orders in Spain besides that of the Cistercians.

The Holy See took the abbey into its protection from the very beginning and continued to confirm the foundation through the centuries.[2]

Queen Leonora,[3] through whose initiative the abbey was founded, was a descendant of Margaret of Scotland through her father, Henry II of England. She was a replica of her mother Eleanor of Aquitaine, one of the greatest figures of the Middle Ages. When the elder daughter Matilda was married at the age of twelve—the usual marriageable age—Leonora became her mother's constant companion for two years and was formed under Eleanor of Aquitaine's knowledgeable guidance and spiritual fervor. At the early age of nine, Leonora was betrothed to the child king Alphonsus of Castile and went to live in Spain. A little later the marriage was celebrated at Burgos with great rejoicing and luxurious pageantry. In the early years of his rule Alphonsus developed—what was unusual at that time—a policy of protection of the Jews, and he displayed a great zeal for the Church. The historian Pistorius attributes these activities to the influence of the young queen, and to this we may add also to the influence of the queen's mother Eleanor, whose untiring and energetic policies formed all Europe. At her residence in Poitiers, her court was the center of art, literature, and music, a land of the troubadors, where the Arthurian legends flourished. It was an age of great faith, and Eleanor's generous patronage of the Order of Fontevrault was the example that inspired the young Leonora to do likewise in founding Las Huelgas de Burgos.

The account of the foundation of the abbey in the Cistercian Annals [4] shows with what care and diligence the new community was made to conform precisely to the traditional customs and ideals of the Cistercian Order. It is necessary to insist on this point because at a later date the custom of abbesses hearing confession, which was practiced at Burgos, was withdrawn as being an abuse. At the first chapter of the foundation three bishops were present: the Bishop of Burgos, the Bishop of Palentinus, and Bishop Martinus of Seguuntius. There were eight abbesses and seven abbots present besides the representative of the General Chapter of the Cistercians of Citaux, Guillimus Scala Dei, for permission to start a new Cistercian Abbey had been requested and granted from headquarters at Citaux.

The Abbey of Las Huelgas was exempt from the jurisdiction of a bishop from 1188 until 1874. In a bull of Urban VIII the abbey is specifically said to be independent of any diocese: *Nullius diocesis.*[5] The first abbess, doña Misol of Tulebras, was chosen from an earlier existing abbey. From the start fifty-two villages and churches were included under the jurisdiction of the abbesses; this number grew in later years to some sixty towns. Owing to the fact that the Monastery of Las Huelgas has been able to preserve many of the documents and also because the monastery was able to maintain its exemption until 1874, we have very full and exact knowledge of the jurisdiction exercised by the abbesses.

The abbesses had the right to confer benefices on the clergy of their own choice and to the churches in their "separated" diocese. The abbesses diocese was called "separated" because it was not dependent on any bishop, and the abbess was herself directly dependent on the Holy See. The abbess had the right to establish new parishes in her territories and to bestow the duty of the "cure of souls" on her clergy. Neither the bishop nor the Apostolic Delegate had the right to visit the churches, the parishes, the clergy, or the beneficiaries in the district under her jurisdiction, even though the sacraments were administered there. In the same way as a bishop the abbess had the right to punish and to summons any priest preaching heresy in her diocese. In the same way as a bishop the abbess had the power to punish lay members in her district, including any from outside the district who committed criminal offenses within. The abbess had the right to unite parishes in her district and to transfer the benefices from one church to another, as for example, from one church that had fallen out of use, to another more active parish. She had the duty of rebuilding dilapidated churches. In the same way as a bishop the abbess promulgated dispensations and graces received from Rome for her district and diocese. She had the right to examine the veracity of cases of public criminals who claimed special pardon. She could establish works of charity and whatsoever institute or hospital she wished in her diocese. She had the right to visit and examine the ability of the Apostolic notaries and also the Imperial or Royal notaries, with the duty of punishing any offense in the execution of their office. The abbess heard matrimonial cases and criminal cases from among her subjects; in the same way as any bishop, she acted through ecclesiastical judges nominated by her. It was the duty of the abbess to approve confessors from among her secular and regular clergy and to examine them for their suitability for their work before nominating them. There was no need for the approbation of the bishop or any other superior. The confessors nominated by the abbess had the right of hearing confession from her subjects and also from visitors or pilgrims within her territory. The confessors could absolve sins reserved to bishops if authorized by the abbess. The abbess had the right of appointing the confessor for the nuns, and neither they nor any lay sisters in obedience to her could go to another confessor without the approval of the abbess.

The abbess had the right through the intermediary of her personally elected ecclesiastical judges to censure and impose interdicts on subjects in her district; she could dispense her clergy from Divine Office when necessary, and she could dispense vows or annul them. The abbess had the right to give permission to her nuns to enter and leave the convent, at a time when in other countries this right had been withdrawn, as at Jouarre and Fontevrault. The abbess had the right to license bishops to exercise pontifical rites within her diocese. She issued licenses to priests giving them the right to say Mass in her churches.

The Abbess Sancha García, the third abbess of Las Huelgas (1207–30) considered she had the right to hear confessions,[6] preach and read the gospel in public, and give the habit to her nuns. This opinion was shared with other Cistercian convents in Spain at Leon and Calhorra, both monasteries subject to Las Huelgas of Burgos. It was evidently a custom they had practiced since the beginning. Knowing the care that was taken by Las Huelgas to conform with the Cistercian Order in France, we can take it that it must have been once an original Cistercian custom. But in 1200 it was considered an abuse, and Innocent III, having been informed about this, sent a bull *Nova Quaedum* prohibiting the continuation of this practice. But while doing so, Innocent III in no way deterred the abbesses from the form of jurisdiction just described, which was then considered quite normal and in no way an abuse. Had it been otherwise, the bull would have been directed against the abbess with regard to her powers of jurisdiction too. This is what the nuns of Conversano pointed out to the King of Naples in 1809, and they knew what they were talking about, for the nuns of Las Huelgas then were still exercising their rights of jurisdiction.

The question of abbesses hearing confession has been treated in Appendix VI. There were three religious rules that gave instructions regarding abbesses hearing confession: the Rule of Donatus to virgins, the *Cuiusdam Regula*, and the Basilian Rule. There are a quantity of stories in the life of Fara, who as abbess of Faremoutier heard the confessions of her community, which according to the Rule of Donatus was held three times a day in private and not as a community chapter admission of faults.

Burganza defended the nuns in his book *Antigüidades de España* and considered the denouncement made against the nuns was similar to that of the Tribune of Inquisition against Saint Teresa of Avila. Manrique considered Constanza—a daughter of Queen Leonora and a nun of Las Huelgas, who possibly held the position of abbess in an interim period—guilty of preaching.[7] Rodríguez does not agree.[8] Bede would not have considered her guilty, had she preached, for he speaks with admiration of women doing so.[9] The reading of the Gospel during the celebration of Matins by the abbess is common today in all women's communities, but in the time of Abbess Sancha García, she would have done so in front of her twenty canons, who may well have attended the Divine Office.

It looks as though the nuns did not immediately agree to the bull of Innocent III, because Innocent IV [10] gave a special privilege to a Cistercian abbot to correct the nuns who went beyond their rights; that is, of hearing confessions from either laity or religious. The Cistercian abbots evidently did not have this right to correct nuns before this date, otherwise there would have been no need for a special privilege to be given by Pope Innocent IV. The Cistercians have only one order, not a first and second order as do the Benedictines, so that the abbesses were on a par with the abbots.

The idea held today that in religious orders a man must necessarily be head over women in the guise of Cardinal protector or abbot of a General Chapter was no more common in Spain than elsewhere in medieval times. There is the example of the double community of Santa Maria de Piasca, which was first under Abbess doña Justa (999) and continued to be under abbesses until 1051. Then an abbot was chosen as head, but by 1058 it was again an abbess who ruled.[11] There was also the community at Covarrubias, not far from Burgos, where today there exists in the archives a Wisigothic document giving the formula of oaths taken by two priests to the abbess on November 25, 979.[12]

The fact, therefore, that King Alphonsus arranged for the Hospital "del Rey," served by a men's military order, to be subject to the abbess of Las Huelgas (built only a short distance from the monastery), was quite a normal system. It was in fact usual for all religious orders to sponsor the charitable running of a hospital for the poor within their territories and under their control. Only at a later date did it create some friction.

THE DEPENDENCE OF THE HOSPITAL "DEL REY" ON THE MONASTERY

As already mentioned, while the foundation of the women's Cistercian abbey was the special initiative of Queen Leonora, the Hospital "del Rey" was the enterprise of the king. The head of the men's community who ran the hospital was not an abbot, he was called a *Comendador,* which can be translated as "prefect," rather than "commander," although of course it was derived from the military term, for these military orders were formed to nurse the wounded in the Crusades. Under him were the *Freyles,* the name given to knights in a military order. The whole hospital or hospice, instituted to look after the poor as well as the sick and the pilgrims on their way to the shrine of Compostella, was subject to the abbess of Las Huelgas.

The *Comendador* and the *Freyles* made their profession in the hands of the abbess. All candidates had to be approved by the abbess. According to the Cistercian Rule, the superiors of the men's division would present the name to the abbess for her approval. After admission and the taking of the habit, there followed a year of probation during which the novice worked in the hospital and cared for the sick. Then, if he were accepted for profession, the following solemn ceremony took place.

The abbess seated on her cathedra in the hospital church of Mary Magdalene with the community of the nuns behind her, held a Missal, the Rule of Saint Benedict, and a crucifix in her hands. The *Frey* knelt before her and placed his hands on the crucifix and on the Rule and on the Missal and pronounced in a loud voice his promise: "I . . . Novice of the Hospital del Rey promise chastity, poverty and obedience till death to God and Our Lord and to the Illustrious lady, my lady . . . who by the grace of God and the Apostolic See is Abbess of the Monastery of Las Huelgas, my Prelate, and my Lady, Superior, Mother and legitimate administrator in spiritual and temporal affairs of the Royal Monastery and its Hospital "del Rey," and of the other Monasteries and affiliations, towns and places under its jurisdiction, Lords and vassals to the future abbesses and superiors, according to the Rule of Saint Benedict and the Order of the Cistercians. And I vow by God and by the writings of the four Gospels, by the doctrine contained therein, as I place my right hand on Christ Crucified, and the book of the Missal, so I promise to accomplish all that has here been said and I vow, as far as I am able, to procure the good of the hospital, its property and estate and to prevent any damage, so I say so I vow. Amen."

After the pronouncing of the vows, the abbess briefly exhorted the newly professed to carry out what he had promised, and she offered her habit to be kissed and gave him her benediction.

The *Comendador* was elected by the brothers and confirmed by the abbess, whom she then formerly commanded to undertake the direction of the brothers by obedience, and she commanded the brothers to obey their *Comendador Major*.

In 1235 Pope Gregory IX confirmed the subjection of the hospital to the abbesses of Las Huelgas.[13] This was further confirmed by bulls of Innocent IV and Paul V.

It was not often necessary for the abbess to actually exercise her rights over the government of the hospital. But on one occasion in the fifteenth century the abbess doña Maria de Guzman considered it her duty to depose the *Comendador* Frey Martin of Salazar.

He was accused of calumny and ordered by the abbess to present himself at the lawcourts, and judgment was passed against him. The abbess informed the *Freyes* and told them to elect another freely and to submit the name to her in the ordinary way.

In the opening paragraph of the letter summoning the *Comendador* Frey Martin de Salazar, the abbess declared herself Mother Superior with jurisdiction in spiritual and temporal matters of the hospital.

The power of the abbess over a man's order and hospital has been considered very extraordinary by modern writers. But in fact as proved in this book it was quite ordinary in many religious orders and in particular women's religious orders, which were the descendants of the communities of deaconesses and who had the duty of caring for the sick, so that hospitals were founded by the side of the monastic foundations. Just to name a few we can mention the Hospital of Saint John at Quedlinburg, which was under the abbess, confirmed by a bull of Alexander III addressed to the abbess *Adelheidis Palatinae*. The abbess was instructed by the pope to see that a priest was appointed to serve the sick of the hospital, granting the right of burial without impediment of excommunication. There were hospitals attached to the convents of Gandersheim, Essen, Gerode, Wetter, and Freckenhurst and to Canoness Institutes in Cologne, Nivelles, Odilienberg, Remiremont, Auxerre in Belgium and others in France. All the hospitals in England were attached to either men's or women's orders before the suppression of monasteries, so much so that when these were suppressed in London in the sixteenth century, there followed four years in which there were no hospitals in London functioning at all.

The explanation for the building of hospitals in the close vicinity of religious orders on which they were dependent was the injunction of Jesus Christ that to obtain the cure of the sick there was need of penance and prayer. Also it is understandable that members of religious orders sought to express their faith both in prayer and charitable works. The connection of hospitals with religious institutes or orders was common both in the East and the West. The famous hospital of Saint Basil was built in the vicinity of the religious community founded by his sister Macrina, who also looked after the hospital. In Constantinople it was the deaconess Olympias, with whom John Chrysostom corresponded, whose community of sisters cared for the sick.

It is this tradition of the natural relationship between religious orders and hospital foundations that explains why the Hospital "del Rey" was dependent on the Monastery of Las Huelgas, and instead of being scandalized about such a thing,[14] we should on the contrary admire the tradition.

THE CULTURE AND SPIRITUALITY OF THE ABBEY

Las Huelgas became very famous for its music. The abbey had a trained choir of young girl singers like the choir of boy singers in cathedral schools. In the time of the Abbess Berenguela, daughter of Ferdinand III and Beatrix (1241–88), the number of choir nuns is given at a hundred and the children who were trained for the choir numbered forty.[15] But the greatest testimony of their musical erudition is to be seen in the *Codex Musical de Las Huelgas*[16] dating from the fourteenth century, copied from an earlier manuscript transcribed by Maria Gonzalez de Aguero about 1325. The manuscript is beautifully and clearly written. The very complicated polyphonic motets and sequences show that the monastery must have had a very highly trained choir in order to sing such musical compositions. The motets in the codex cover the widest possible repertory of the most ancient tunes and give evidence of contact with schools of music in many different countries, such as the schools at Notre-Dame, Paris, and Montpellier in France, besides those in Germany and other parts of Spain. Today the codex is studied by all historians of music as giving the earliest examples of polyphonic chants.

The life of doña Antonia Jacinta de Novarra, a nun of Las Huelgas who lived in the seventeenth century at the time of the famous Abbess Anna of Austria, throws light on customs of the community.

Jacinta was born at Pamplona on December 10, 1602. Her

mother doña Leonor Eriques de Cueva was of the Duchy of Alburquerque; her father Felipe de Navarra and Cueva was a descendant of Carlos II. Jacinta was the first of eight children.

Jacinta [17] was very precocious; at the age of five she was like a girl of ten. An aunt, a sister of her father, was a member of the community of Las Huelgas at Burgos, and a sister of her mother was a Carmelite. It was understandable that she decided early that she wanted to become a nun. However, her parents were very against the idea.

One day Jacinta had a vision of her aunt standing together with the Virgin Mary and two angels on either side of her, and Jacinta called those in the house to come to see, but the vision disappeared. Eight days later, it was reported that the aunt at Las Huelgas had died.

Jacinta was seven and a half years old when she was taken to live with many other girls of royal families in the school conducted at the Convent of Las Huelgas. In August 1609, on the Feast of the Assumption, she solemnly received the habit worn by all other schoolgirls. The children followed mitigated rules of the novices. Jacinta learned to read, write, and sing; she played musical instruments and studied Christian doctrine. She imitated the hermits by hiding herself away in solitary places and spent many hours in front of a statue of the Virgin. She was specially attracted to the prayer of "Our Father," and she developed the desire to become a discalced Carmelite and asked her parents to let her leave Las Huelgas to join the Carmelites. But all this was looked upon as a caprice of youth.

At this period the ruling was introduced that the election of abbesses was to take place every three years instead of for life. Anna of Austria, daughter of don Juan of Austria, the hero of the battle of Lepanto, was elected abbess. The ceremony of her installation was performed with elaborate medieval rite. Philip III and all the royal court assisted. A lighter side to the festivity was allowed by the staging of a comic play enacted by the child-novices of the abbey. Antonia Jacinta was chosen to direct the show and to play a part in it.[18] She was so successful, graceful, and attractive that one of the knights fell in love with her at first sight and asked her to be his wife. Jacinta energetically refused his advances by emitting a piercing scream, which brought her companions to her side and preserved her from further embarrassment.

Two of her companions, unlike herself, had decided to get married and counseled her to do likewise. Jacinta had read all the novels, poems, and songs of her day; she was passionately fond of acting. However, she had made up her mind to enter religious life. She practiced fasting without letting it be known, by hiding food under the table and taking only bread and water. At the age of fourteen she fell ill. She had what she called diabolical temptations. She saw knights with elegant hands, and when bothered by these things she told the nuns; they looked down upon her. Just before her profession she had a more comforting vision. She saw a spacious field and Our Lord passing through it, which filled her with great emotion, so that she could not eat and became ill and was thought to be dying. By request of the Abbess Anna of Austria a picture of the Virgin Mary was brought to Jacinta's room, and she was given Extreme Unction. She suddenly sat up and recovered.

From the age of seventeen to thirty, Antonia Jacinta experienced the pains of the Passion every Friday, with wounds that appeared on her feet and side and on her head. During the day she was prostrate in her room and unable to eat or take part in community functions; but for the rest of the week she attended Divine Office regularly with the others. By order of the abbess she was told to pray for a lessening of these mystical occurrences. From the age of thirty, although still feeling the pains of the wounds on Fridays, she was able to accompany the community in prayer.

The sisters judged her hypocritical, deceived and misled by the devil, which caused Jacinta great hardship. Eventually, however, the community became convinced of her integrity and of the authenticity of her mystical experiences, so much so that in old age she was even chosen as abbess. Her confessor requested her to write a full account of her experiences, which she did.[19] These have been declared doctrinally and morally free of error. Her work has never been published, but the manuscript is kept in the archives of the abbey for anyone who might have the interest and the ardor to copy out her long handwritten pages. The members of the Cistercian Order today, who continue to function at Burgos, fight shy of making Jacinta known, feeling that such exceptional spirituality can be of little help and perhaps a danger to novices. For those who have studied mystical phenomena, her book would be a mine of information.

After her death she was declared venerable, but was never beatified.

It was during the regime of the Abbess Anna of Austria that the bull *Inscrutabili* was issued by Gregory XV, on February 5, 1622, in Rome. It chiefly concerned the choice of confessors and preachers in parishes and in the churches of religious orders. It was intended to correct abuses that were then prevalent. In order to effect these reforms, Gregory XV required the bishop's approval of confessors and preachers, not only for the parishes but also for religious orders, including orders that were ordinarily exempt from episcopal jurisdiction. The bishops had always been called on to ordain the clergy of orders that had exemption, and to approve the confessors and preachers was perhaps not looked upon by the pope as a revoking of the rights of *Nullius Diocesis*. Luther's thesis on indulgences and his accusation of abuses provoked by confessors may have led the Council of Trent to take this forceful method to counteract such things. Since the right of hearing confession by the abbesses and the right to preach had been taken away by Innocent III, women's religious orders were particularly in danger of being undermined by unscrupulous confessors, and scandals could all the more easily arise.

The bull was not intended however to suppress the quasi-episcopal jurisdiction. This is proved by the bull of Urban VIII to Anna of Austria in 1629.[20] She had written to him for information regarding the interpretation of the bull *inscrutabili* and certain decrees of the Council of Trent. He wrote assuring her that the Constitutions and Regulations of the decrees of the Council of Trent did not repudiate her authority, and he confirmed her privileges of immunity, liberty, and exemption, emphasizing both her spiritual and temporal jurisdiction and declared her of *Nullius diocesis Ordinis Cisterciensis*. The monastery of Las Huelgas de Burgos had no further difficulties with bishops, for this clear statement of complete exemption made their position quite secure.

NAPOLEON IN SPAIN

Las Huelgas suffered like other religious orders at the time of the occupation of Spain by Napoleon, but with less drastic effects than in Italy or France. By an alliance between Spain and France on October 1, 1800, Napoleon was made President of the Consulate and entered Burgos on April 29, 1801. He remained in power until March 19, 1809. King Charles IV of Spain was obliged to abdicate in favor of his son Ferdinand VII who was in the power of Napoleon.[21]

In the preceding Battle of Burgos, there had been eighteen thousand Spanish military against Napoleon's forty thousand; the French took possession of the royal abbey and made it their barracks. Three old nuns refused to leave and were allowed to remain. The invaders pillaged all they could in the abbey and the hospital. They profaned the sepulchres of the royalty and took jewels and diamonds from the tomb of doña Constanza, daughter of Alphonsus VIII and Leonora of England. They stole eight chalices, six candlesticks, three crosses, and they took dinner sets used for royal visits. They got some of the precious manuscripts and documents in the archives of the abbey, but luckily not all. The nuns had hidden many in the double walls of the building, and these were not found, so that today there is still a very considerable number to be consulted and which have been carefully catalogued for the use of historians.

After the fall of Napoleon in 1815, the nuns returned to the abbey and continued to run the Hospital "del Rey," with the generous financial help of both Alphonsus XII and Alphonsus XIII. Under Abbess Isabel II, the abbey returned to its former conditions and still retained its quasi-episcopal jurisdiction together with twelve dependent houses, differing from Italy, where the women's religious orders never recovered their former jurisdiction.

The Monastery of Las Huelgas and the twelve dependent convents continued for another half century to maintain the same spiritual and temporal jurisdiction. The following formula of a license issued by the Abbess Bernarda Ruiz Puente to a priest don Pedro Orena to say Mass in her district is an example of their pastoral care. The first paragraph was common to all and then was followed by the particular case in question:

We Bernarda Ruiz Puente, by the grace of God and the Holy Apostolic See, Abbess of the Royal Monastery of Las Huelgas, in vicinity of the town of Burgos, of the Cistercian Order, in conformity with our Father Saint Bernard, Lady, Superior, Prelate, Mother and legitimate administrator in spiritual matters of the said Royal Monastery and its Hospital, called that of "the king," and of the convents, churches and hermitages of its affiliated institutes, in virtue of the bulls and warrants and apostolic grants, with complete jurisdiction, exclusive, quasi-episcopal, *Nullius Diocesis.*

We acknowledge the evidence of Don Pedro Orena's ability and capacity to be priest, chaplain and head sacristan of the Hospital of the King, following the rubrics, feast days and the Masses and events that therein occur, we give him license, that wearing long vestments, he may celebrate in the church of the Monastery and all other churches, hospitals and hermitages of our District, in the institutions of our affiliations and under our jurisdiction, for so long as we may desire, and we prescribe that the rubrics and ceremonies be carried out with precision. Specially it is required that the Holy and Solemn Sacrifice of the Mass shall be conducted with due length of time, gravity and composure and decorum corresponding to the majesty and magnitude of so an august ministry, taking at least a third part of an hour at the altar, in conformity with the instructions published in various edicts by Rome, particularly the one sent on 9th August 1734 by his Holiness Clement XII, and we hereby give the present signature, sealed with the seal of our abacial dignity and legalized by the underwritten secretary, within the accountancy office of the Royal Monastery of Las Huelgas, near Burgos, the 26th March 1864.

Bernarda Ruiz Puente Abbess.
By the command of her Eminence the Lady Abbess, Roman Pocheco. Not. Srio.[22]

Ten years later (1873) the bull *quae diversa*[23] of Pius IX issued from Rome brought to an end all quasi-episcopal jurisdiction in Spain in both men and women's orders, due to the change of times. It took a year before it was put into effect at Las Huelgas.

Pius IX explained that with the change of civil society, the custom used by the Church of giving exemption from episcopal jurisdiction to various institutes was now inopportune, if not harmful, and so it was now necessary to abolish the special privileges of quasi-episcopal jurisdiction in both men's and women's orders. The name of Las Huelgas was not mentioned in particular, but only all women's orders in general. The only order mentioned by name was that of Saint James of Jerusalem. All institutes were to be put under the jurisdiction of the bishop of the diocese in which the houses were situated; this corresponds to the main point of the *Concordat* arranged between Pius VII and Napoleon, and which was still in force.

Cardinal Juan Ignacio Moreno, Archbishop of Valladolid, was commissioned by the pope to see that the bull was put into effect. A letter was sent to the Abbess of Las Huelgas asking her for a detailed account of her territories, people and parishes, notaries, benefices, clergy and chaplains, the list of the monasteries of religious orders and all pious institutes that were situated within the precincts of the diocese and subject to the Abbey of Las Huelgas, and he asked for all documents justifying their exemption and what it actually entailed.

On October 7, 1873, the abbess sent a forceful defense of the privileges of Las Huelgas prepared by the Canon Penitentiary of the Cathedral of Burgos, Don Tiburcio Rodríguez, to Pope Pius IX.

In her letter it was sustained that the bull *Quae diversa* did not mention the name of the Abbey of Las Huelgas, and as the indult of the quasi-episcopal jurisdiction was given directly from the Holy See, it would be necessary that the monastery be expressly named, and the regular prelates could not be expected to forfeit their jurisdiction and their rights of exemption with quasi-episcopal power without a direct injunction from the Holy See. The letter then recalls the bulls of the former popes, from Clement III in 1197 and 1188, in which the foundation was approved and made dependent on the Holy See. It made reference to the confirmations of Honorius III, September 11, 1219; of Gregory IX, July 20, 1234; of Innocent IV, April 29, 1246; of Innocent VIII, July 30, 1487 and August 13, 1489; of Leo X, June 1, 1521; of

Urban VIII addressed to the Abbess Anna of Austria, confirming all privileges of the past both spiritual and temporal; and of that of October 2, 1632, confirming all exemptions, privileges, and grants conceded to her antecedents. The bull of Pius IX referred to the exemption of prelates of regular orders, of which the Abbess of Las Huelgas was one being of the First Order of the Cistercians, and so again a specific mention of the Monastery of Las Huelgas would be required if it were intended to be included within the bull.

On January 20, 1874, Cardinal Moreno gave the reasons why the bull *Quae diversa* was to be interpreted as covering the Monastery of Las Huelgas and declared the quasi-episcopal jurisdiction of Las Huelgas suppressed. Don Jose de Arteaga, the Vicar General of the Archbishop of Burgos, was delegated to take over the monastery in the name of the archbishop. He presented himself first at the accountancy office and then at the sacristy and church.

The Abbess and the community, although very upset, accepted the loss of status with Christian resignation. On February 1, 1874, the abbess addressed letters to the twelve affiliated abbeys informing them that their right of exemption had been suppressed and advising them to comply with the wishes of the Church.

Amancio Lopez Rodríguez, author of the two volumes on the Abbey of Las Huelgas, expressed his opinion on the suppression as an immense misfortune. He declared his admiration for the spirit of abnegation displayed by the nuns in accepting the decree.

CONCLUSION

It is obvious that the status of the quasi-episcopal abbesses has been whittled away slowly over the centuries. The Mozarabic *Liber Ordinum*, which was used up to the eleventh century in Spain, provided the tradition for ordained abbesses, with no discrimination of sexes. It is understandable that the abbesses of the Cistercian Abbeys thought they had the right to hear confessions, preach, and read the Gospel in public. When that right was taken away by Innocent III in the thirteenth century on the grounds that it was an abuse, there was no question of the abbess's jurisdiction over all the churches, clergy, and people within her "separated" district being wrong. This tradition was, on the contrary, upheld by the Holy See over many centuries; it was clearly defined by Pope Urban VIII in his bull to the Abbess Anna of Austria, in which he confirmed her spiritual and temporal jurisdiction and addressed her as being of *Nullius diocesis ordinis Cisterciensis.* When Pius IX decided to withdraw this right of jurisdiction, he did not have the courage to write directly to the abbeys.

All this is now hidden history.

CHAPTER TEN

HOW THE QUASI-EPISCOPAL ABBESSES LOST STATUS

I T HAS BEEN PROVED that the true Christian tradition regarding the participation of women in the service of the Church has been hidden. The early inscriptions of *Episcopa, Sacerdos Maxima, Sacerdotes Virgines, Praeposita, diaconissa,* are substantiated by the early ordination rites. The many Canoness Institutes and religious orders with abbesses holding jurisdiction over the churches, the clergy, and the people within their "separated" districts gives indisputable evidence that women have been traditionally appointed to the administration of the Church. The fact that the papacy upheld their rights through so many centuries can be understood when it is realized that these traditions were held from "immemorial" times. There are proofs that early Christian law, such as the Code of Justinian, sought to bring about greater equality between the sexes. The lives of the empresses of the Byzantine Empire and of European queens such as Margaret of Scotland testify to the acceptance of women as rulers, including of Church affairs.

It was the return to a pagan Greco-Roman culture that brought about a return to a low evaluation of women. By the sixteenth century the opinion of Aristotle vied with that of Christ. It was only at this time that monks began to think they could not be in obedience to a woman. Leadership took on the pagan character of patriarchal domination instead of the Christian ideal of humble service. Women were turned out of professions and trades, and they were turned out of the service of the Church.

The Reformation returned to a Hebrew and Old Testament evaluation of women, which allowed her a position in the home but in subservience to her husband. It was John Knox who, in his subversive pamphlet "The First Blast of the Trumpet, against the Monstrous Regiment of Women," revived the idea that women had no right to rule over men.[1] This was quite contrary to the idea of the Middle Ages as seen at the Foundation of Fontevrault. There the idea of the vow of obedience taken by clergy and monks, besides the nuns, to the abbess was considered a highly commendable act. It did not occur to the clergy or monks that it was below them to take a vow to a woman until well into the fifteenth century. Then a new formula for the clergy was arranged by which a priest made the vow to the abbess with the consent of the bishop, which had not been considered necessary before. It was not until the sixteenth century that the priests and monks definitely planned independence of the abbess. In the lawsuit brought up by the monks against the nuns, they repeated John Knox's phrase that it was against nature and against God for a man to be in obedience to a woman. The judges, however, confirmed the authority of the abbess as it was an age-long practice. It was at the basis of the spirituality of the order—a spirituality based on the imitation of Christ who obeyed his mother. Authority, according to Christian doctrine, did not permit one person to dominate another, but entailed service— humble service. All this was forgotten and changed by the return of Greco-Roman and Hebrew ideas of male predominance.

By the time of the Council of Trent,[2] the new attitude toward women, due to the Renaissance and the Reformation, had affected all society, including Church authorities. At the last session of the Council of Trent, December 25, 1563, decisions were made regarding the reformation of religious orders. Strict enclosure was enforced on women's orders. No nun was allowed out of the convent grounds without the approval of the bishop. This rule was to apply to exempt orders, so overriding the jurisdiction of the quasi-episcopal abbesses.

Yet before the Council of Trent the Abbess Maria de Bretagne had already reformed the Abbey of Fontevrault, and her example had been followed by other orders, including the Abbey of Jouarre. The Council's legislation was uncalled for.

The Council ordered women's monasteries that were not already part of a General Chapter of a Congregation to join with one. This gave power to the head of the men's congregation over the women's. If they did not do so within a year after the end of the council, the metropolitan bishop was held responsible, as delegate of the Apostolic See, to convoke the monasteries for the purpose of forming congregations. This meant that abbesses who were independent of any bishop—that is, with quasi-episcopal jurisdiction—were now forced to accept their nearest bishop, not as bishop—so not legally violating the age-old privilege—but as delegate of the Holy See.

The idea that women superiors should necessarily come under the higher hierarchical male superior was not approved by all bishops of the Council of Trent.[3] The Abbot Stephen of the Order of Saint Cassain wanted to remove the rule regarding nuns being under the supervision of monks. But the last session was hurriedly closed with little time for discussion.

Although numbers of abbesses held episcopal jurisdiction for many centuries, it was not until 1638 that a theologian, Tamburini,[4] produced a complete treatise on the nature of the authority of the abbesses. With a lawyer's dexterity he sought to explain it away.

In *Disputatio XXXII, Quasitum II*[5] he questioned whether it was possible for an abbess to have spiritual jurisdiction, even though many papal bulls recognized both spiritual and civil jurisdiction as held by the abbesses of exempt abbeys. Tamburini asserted that as the abbess could not hold the power of the priesthood, she could not have spiritual jurisdiction that he maintained was connected with the power of the "keys," and so was part of the sacrament of priesthood. He further asserted that the abbess as a religious belonged to the laity and that she could not hold spiritual jurisdiction nor spiritual understanding.

This view was not upheld by the canonist and historian Van Espen, who, approximately a century later, produced a study on the power of the abbesses in his comprehensive work *Jus ecclesiasticum*, in which he devoted a whole chapter to canonesses.[6] He had collected some interesting traditions of long standing, in particular with regard to the canonesses of Belgium at Mons, Malbordió, Namur, Arden, and Nivelles. Van Espen quoted from the works of Bertrandus Loth, *Resolutionibus Belgias*,[7] in which the churches of the canonesses were mentioned as recognized by the bishops of the locality and that these were not considered as private chapels belonging to an order, but as parishes belonging to the diocese. The canonesses took part in the ecclesiastical processions and had a place among the clergy. The abbesses had the honor of leading the processions carrying a pastoral cross and vested in ecclesiastical robes of prelates.

Van Espen further proved the importance of the abbesses of Canoness Institutes by the fact that many were summoned to local synods. In 1565 among the signatures of the Synod of Cambrais were the names of Margaret de Hinkaert, Abbess of Malbodio and Margaret of Noyelles, Abbess of Nivelles. These two abbeys were royal and so did not come under the new legislation of the Council of Trent.

The French Revolution, with its motto "Fraternity, Liberty and Equality," might be expected to have been beneficial to women. Indeed, French women did hope so; between 1789 and 1793 many women's unions were formed claiming equality of the sexes in political and social issues.[8] But the revolutionary women's societies were roughly treated by the male leaders of the French Revolution. In 1791 Olympe de Gouge, an exceptional woman of the French Revolution, presented Queen Marie Antoinette with a declaration demanding that women citizens should be allowed to vote. When she dared to oppose Robespierre for his reign of terror, she herself was sent to the guillotine. And Rose Lacombe[9] likewise attacked Robespierre's cruelty in an intrepid speech and was brought to court and her mouth held when she sought to defend herself. Subsequently all women's societies were suppressed.

By the persecution of the nobility during the French Revolution women lost the high positions they often had held as members of ruling families. But the rough and barbaric male leaders of the revolution were not prepared to accept women in the new democratic regime. This was fought for later on.

As a result of the suppression of religious orders through the French Revolution, women lost their chief centers of education. The advent of the Napoleonic Empire was only to do women further damage.[10] The *Code Civil* placed wives in complete subordination to their husbands in a way worse than in Roman classical and pagan paternalistic times. The *Concordat* with Rome allowed religious property to remain in the hands of the government. Some redress was made by means of the government salaries for the clergy. No provision was made for the nuns who had likewise lost their property. The subordination of all remaining religious orders to the pro-Napoleonic bishops established by Napoleon put an end to the administration of exempt abbeys held by either abbots or quasi-episcopal abbesses. Only Las Huelgas de Burgos and the twelve dependent abbeys were able to re-establish themselves after the defeat of Napoleon. In other countries, his rule had been too long for the dispersed monasteries to reassert themselves. Where nuns were able to gather together again they did so under the jurisdiction of the bishops.

Finally, as it has been told, Pius IX took away the right of the Spanish Abbesses to exemption on the grounds that with the change of regime the system was no longer in keeping with the new democratic ideas. At that time democracy did not include women, so one half of the human race was left out.

THE TABOO OF WOMEN DURING PREGNANCY AND MENSTRUATION

A TABOO AGAINST WOMEN during pregnancy and menstruation was common among many nations in early pre-Christian centuries. It was legislated for in the Hebrew code in Leviticus and carried through into Christian times, and it lasted over very many centuries. Not only were women considered to be "impure" during these periods, but in danger of communicating their impurity to others. This factor, more than any other, has been the cause of the ostracizing of womankind—impeding them from participating in social, political, and religious meetings.

THE TABOO AMONG ZOROASTRIANS

The Zoroastrians, whose religious culture covered vast areas of Iran through to India, have certainly played a large part in the propagation of these ideas. They believed that the menses was caused by the evil god Ahriman. A woman during menstruation was considered unclean and possessed of a demon. She had to be kept confined and apart from the people so that she would not touch or degrade them. Her very look could, they thought, injure and defile fire. Therefore, of course, she was not able to take part in the ceremonies of the sacred fire. To this day a room for the monthly seclusion of women, bare of all comforts, is set aside in the Parsee house, where moon and stars and sun cannot penetrate.[1] Among the ancient Zoroastrians women were considered unclean also during pregnancy and childbirth.[2]

TABOO IN CLASSICAL TIMES

The opinion of more civilized ancient societies was very little better than the primitive ones. Pliny gives us the information that contact with the monthly flux of women turns new wine sour, makes crops wither, kills grafts, dries seeds in gardens, causes the fruit of trees to fall off, dims the bright surface of mirrors, dulls the edge of steel and the gleam of ivory, kills bees, rusts iron and bronze, and causes a horrible smell to fill the air. Dogs who taste the blood become mad, and their bite becomes poisonous as in rabies. The Dead Sea, thick with salt, cannot be drawn asunder except by a thread soaked in the poisonous fluid of the menstruous blood. A thread from an infected dress is sufficient. Linen, touched by the woman while boiling and washing it in water, turns black. So great is the power of women that they say that hailstorms and whirlwinds are driven away if menstrual fluid is exposed to the flashes of lightning. Wild indeed are the stories told of the mysterious and awful discharge itself, the manifold magic of which is great. If this female power should issue when the moon or sun is in eclipse it will cause irremediable harm. At such seasons sexual intercourse brings disease and death on the man.[3]

In the Hindu Brahmanas, in spite of all the prayers for a son, when a woman is with child she is considered impure. She is forbidden to go to the assembly. The Maitareya Samhita ranks her as inferior to a bad man and describes her as one of the major evils in human society.[4]

The Chinese Buddhists have the same taboo today with regard to women during their period of menstruation. Kin Tran-Thi, a Buddhist from the northern Vietnamese, who with her family migrated south and has since settled in Europe, and who has a nursing degree, tells me that from generation to generation women are taught not to approach the Buddhist altar nor to burn incense to the tablets of the ancestors during their monthly periods. A woman with child, however, is not regarded as impure, which is at least a little more rational, as it is evident that the main aim is to procure hygienic cleanliness. Clara Leung, a student nurse from Hong Kong, also informs me that after the birth of a child the mother must wait a hundred days before approaching the Buddhist altar. The Jains have the same injunctions not to go to the temple for prayer at the time of menstruation. It is looked on by women as a welcome time of rest. That indeed would have been quite all right had it really been the reason, but it is clear from the customs of the Zoroastrians, the Hebrews, and the many other tribes mentioned that it was not just a hygienic legislation, but a prohibition based on the idea of woman being in contact with the evil one; that is, under the influence of the devil during menstruation.

THE TABOO AMONG HEBREWS

The very many rules regarding impurity in the Torah and other Hebrew books are all interpretations of the Old Testament book: Leviticus 15:19–30.

When a woman has a discharge of blood, and blood flows from her body, the uncleanness of her monthly periods shall last for seven days. Anyone who touches her will be unclean until evening.

Any bed she lies on in this state will be unclean; any seat she sits on will be unclean.

Anyone who touches her bed must wash his clothing and wash himself and will be unclean until evening. If there is anything on the bed or on the chair on which she sat, anyone who touches it will be unclean until evening.

If a man sleeps with her, he will be affected by the uncleanness of her monthly periods. He shall be unclean for seven days. Any bed he lies on will be unclean.

If a woman has a flow of blood for several days outside her period or if the period is prolonged, during the time the flow lasts she shall be in the same state of uncleanness as during her monthly periods.

When she is cured of her flow, she will let seven days pass then she will be clean. On the eighth day she is to take two turtle doves or two young pigeons and bring them to the priest at the entrance of the Tent of Meeting. With one of them the priest is to offer a sacrifice for sin and with the other a holocaust. This is the way in which the priest will perform the rite of atonement over her before Yahweh for the flow that caused her uncleanness.

The sons of Israel are to be warned lest they defile the tabernacle that is set among them.

The more precise way of carrying out the laws in the Leviticus is explained in the Torah. II Tohoreth 7 Mishnah I says: If a man who dwelt in the same courtyard with an Ha-arez, forgot some vessels in the courtyard, even though they were jars with tightly fitting covers, they are deemed unclean for the jars may have been shifted by his menstruant wife.[5]

If the wife of an 'am-Ha-arez entered a Harber's house without his permission to take out his son or daughter, or his cattle, the house remains clean even though she has entered it without permission,[6] but she has to hurry so as not to touch anything.

If a piece of dough that has suffered first grade of uncleanness were made to adhere to another piece, all becomes unclean in the first grade.[7]

Cloth is susceptible to five forms of uncleanness.[8]

The Code of the Maimonides in Book 10 gives very lengthy instructions as to what renders a couch or seat unclean:

The couch or saddle of one who had intercourse with a menstruant is not like the couch or saddle of a menstruant, for the couch or saddle on which the menstruant has pressed is one of the Father of uncleanness; but the couch or saddle of him who has intercourse with a menstruant is but an offspring of the uncleanness, like utensils that he has touched, which do not convey uncleanness to persons or to other utensils, but only to foodstuffs and liquids.[9]

THE TABOO IN THE EARLY CHRISTIAN CHURCH

There is plentiful evidence that the Old Testament injunctions regarding the impurity of women during pregnancy and menstruation were carried over into New Testament times. In the

Eastern and Russian Orthodox churches, and the Ethiopian Orthodox church, the Old Testament legislation still holds good today. In the West the Christian Church retained prohibitions along the same line in Canon Law, although differing in various places, which did not become completely obsolete until the sixteenth century.

Two outstanding documents, one in the East, and one in the West, were contrary to maintaining the rulings of Leviticus. In the East, the *Didascalia and Apostolic Constitutions*[10] has a clause defending women against any imputation of sin during their natural monthly discharge. In the West, the letter of Gregory the Great to Saint Augustine of Canterbury,[11] in reply to a question on this point, insists that women shall not be deprived of entrance into a church nor refused Communion during their monthly periods, or during pregnancy.

The *Didascalia and Apostolic Constitutions* refers to the occasion in the Gospel when the women suffering from hemorrhage was cured by her touching the fringe of Christ's gown,[12] and adds that she was not reprehended for doing so, but on the contrary commended for it and comments that the act merited her cure and remission of sins; furthermore the injunction is given to husbands telling them "when your wives have the natural flow, do not go against them, but sustain them knowing they are members of your own body, love them as your own soul."

Augustine of Canterbury wrote to Pope Gregory I asking him many questions, to which he received a likewise lengthy reply. The letter was brought to him by Melitus, when he was sent on the second mission to England. It is dated 601.[13]

Among the questions regarding women Augustine asked: Was a pregnant woman to be baptized? How long must a woman wait before entering a church after childbirth? During the time of a woman's menstruation may she enter a church and take Communion?

Gregory answers: Why should a pregnant woman not be baptized? It would be ridiculous to see any contradiction between the gift of fertility she has received from God and the gift of grace received at baptism. Regarding entrance into a church after childbirth, he says she is not to be prohibited. So also regarding the period of menstruation, she is likewise not to be prohibited from entering a church, for he adds: the natural flux that she suffers cannot be imputed to her as a fault, therefore it is right that she should not be deprived of the entrance into a church. He too refers to the Gospel story, and says: we know, moreover, that the woman suffering from flux, after she had touched humbly the fringe of Our Lord's dress, was cured immediately. So if this woman may touch Our Lord's dress, and it is told as a laudable thing, why should a menstruating woman not enter church? Nor is she to be prohibited from taking Communion at this time. If the woman out of veneration of the Sacrament does not go, she is to be praised, but if she does go to Communion she is not to be judged adversely. She has no sin. People see sin where there is none. We all eat when hungry, and without sin in doing so, even though it is through the sin of the first man that we are hungry. So women when menstruous have no sin; it is natural.

In spite of this clear and reasonable letter of Gregory, when Theodore of Tarsus was consecrated Bishop of Canterbury in 668 by Pope Vitalian of Rome, Theodore gave England Penitentiary regulations under his own name. In Chapter 9, number 17, he returned to the usual Eastern custom: women during the time of menstruation shall not enter a church nor shall they communicate, neither nuns nor laity shall presume to do so. If they do they are to be given the penance of three days fasting.[14]

Bede, when he wrote his church history in 731,[15] should have known about Theodore's Penitential, but he does not mention it. On the contrary, he mentions the reply given by Gregory I to Augustine allowing women to enter church and to communicate during their periods. The question is asked whether Theodore's Penitential did not reach Bede. This is considered unlikely. Some think that interpolations could have been made in Theodore's canons. Others think Bede did not agree with them. Gregory had been a Benedictine monk, and Bede was himself one, so he would have given far more credence to Gregory rather than to Theodore.

Gregory's opinion was certainly not looked upon as an *ex cathedra* pronouncement. In England as well as on the Continent, women were prohibited to enter a church or to Communicate at these times. After Gratian there was a mitigation of the law,[16] although it differed from place to place. At the Synod of Meaux,[17] France, entrance to the church was not to be denied to women, but it was said to be better if they did not come. And yet in 1572 there is a canon against women going to communion for some time after the birth of a child.

The following opinions of the theologians and doctors of the Christian Church show how widespread was Old Testament legislation on the "impurity" of women:

Saint Jerome, commenting on Zacharias says: "nothing is so unclean as a woman in her periods, what she touches she causes to become unclean." [18] In a letter he also demanded continence before the taking of the Eucharist.[19] Saint Augustine likewise prescribed continence as a preparation for baptism.[20] In a commentary of Ezekiel he says that defective children result from conception taking place while the woman is having her menses. Isidore of Seville (c. 636) in his *etymologiae* says that if fruit is touched by an "unclean" woman it cannot ripen and the plant dies. If dogs partake of menstruous blood, they contract rabies. Caesarius of Arles mentioned in his commentary of Ezekiel that the injunctions of the Old Testament regarding "impurity" still held good in the New Testament. Archbishop Raban Maurus (c. 856) and Bishop Sighard of Cremona (c. 1215) and Innocent III (c. 1216) all continue to quote the opinion of Isidore of Seville as mentioned above. The Bolognese Canonist Rufinus in 1200 speaks of *exsecrabilis et immundus sanguinis*. The penitentiaries of the eighth to the eleventh centuries would not allow women or nuns to enter church or to communicate during their periods. Still as late as 1684 women were told to remain at the door of the church and not to enter.[21]

Although eventually the Church in the West gave way to women's participation in the Sacraments at all times, there is no doubt that it was this prohibition in the early centuries of Christianity that had made it impossible for women to be ordained as priests or to serve at the altar. The clerical ministry of deaconess was only permitted to women at the age of sixty when women had passed the menopause and the possibility of the contagion of impurity.

There are canons that make this quite clear. For example, in the *Liber Legum Ecclesiasticarum*, an English Penitential law book, women are told not to approach the altar during Mass, but to remain in their places in church, and the priest, it is said, will go there and receive from them the oblation they wish to offer to God. The reason given is that women must remember their infirmity and the weakness of their sex, and they must be careful not to render impure any of the things that pertain to the ministry of the church.[22] (The offering was accepted notwithstanding the risk of impurity!)

THE STATUS OF WOMEN IN THE GOSPELS

WOMEN ARE NOT COUNTED in the account of the miracle of the multiplication of loaves. Three of the Evangelists do not mention them at all and state only the number of men.[1] Had it not been for Saint Matthew we would not have known there had been any women present at all. But it made the miracle more sensational to add, as Saint Matthew did, that there were five thousand men not reckoning women and children.[2]

The Evangelists wrote according to the mentality of their age; if women are left out of their accounts it does not mean that they were not there. If all emphasis was given to the Twelve, which anyhow was a number symbolic of the whole Jewish people, it does not mean that women were not included.

Luke alone gives us a clear picture of the group of women who accompanied Our Lord and the Twelve in the missionary tours through the towns and villages of Galilee.[3] All four Evangelists, however, mention the group of women who had followed Jesus from Galilee to Jerusalem at the time of his Passion.[4]

It is Luke who mentions an interesting detail. It was the women who provided for the apostles out of their own resources.[5] In

Latin texts the line reads the women provided for him (*ei*) as though they looked after Jesus alone. But in the Greek texts the words *autois*, for "them" is used. So here we learn that women by the invitation of Jesus traveled about with the Twelve. The mother of the sons of Zebedee was not expected to stay at home; she went with her two sons and left the father in his fishing boat.[6] The group of women had sufficient income to provide for the apostles out of their own resources.

Among the women who followed Jesus in Galilee and who were present at his Passion and who were the first to see him at the Resurrection, nine are mentioned by name. These are: Mary, the mother of Jesus; Mary, the wife of Cleophas; Mary Magdalene, who is mentioned by all four evangelists; Joanna, the wife of Herod's steward Chuza; Susanna, who is not mentioned elsewhere in the Gospels; the mother of the sons of Zebedee; Salome; Mary, the mother of James; and Mary, the mother of James the younger and Joset.[7]

Some of the names are considered a duplication. Mary, the mother of James the younger and Joset may be the same as Mary, the mother of James. Salome may be the same as the mother of the sons of Zebedee. But there is no certainty.

Did this group of women constitute a parallel to the Twelve? There is a mosaic in the *Titulus* Church of Saint Praxedis that suggests it. There is a double circle around the doorway of the chapel of Saint Zeno consisting of the busts of the apostles with Jesus in the center and of the busts of eight women together with Our Lady in the center and two deacons on either side of her. It certainly gives the impression of a tradition of a collateral group of apostles, of men and women.[8]

Jesus was not afraid to go against Jewish customs, even though it shocked the apostles when he spoke to the Samaritan woman at the well.[9] It is the longest private conversation recorded in the Gospels. Jesus declared openly for the first time, and that to a woman, that he was the Messiah. When she asked him in what place God should be worshiped, Jesus did not tell her not to bother about liturgical questions and to leave that to men; on the contrary, he gave her a full and satisfying answer, telling her that God is a spirit, not to be worshiped in Jesusalem nor Samaria, but that those who worship must worship in spirit and truth.

It is to another woman, Mary, the sister of Lazarus, that Jesus revealed the greatest and most astonishing mystery—that he himself is the Resurrection and that those who believe in him, although they die, shall live.[10]

The teaching of Jesus on marriage required a complete change of attitude on the part of the disciples. It was so drastic that they remarked that it was better not to get married at all. A new equality of the sexes was established, both men and women are likewise guilty of sin if either seeks divorce to marry another. But adultery is no longer to be punished by stoning as required by the law of Moses, for it fell only on women.[11] The hypocrisy of men legislating to punish an adulteress, although guilty themselves, was made evident.

To appreciate the change that took place in the position of women in marriage it is necessary to see what was the prevailing rabbinical teaching at the time. There were two schools: the school of Shammai, and the school of Hillel. The school of Shammai taught that transgression of chastity was the sole legitimate cause for seeking divorce, while the school of Hillel allowed divorce for trivial misdemeanors such as the wife having burned the food when cooking. The rabbi Aquila held that if a man found another woman fairer than his own wife, he was justified in dissolving the marriage on the grounds that his first wife "found no favor in his eyes." [12]

Christ honored marriage by using it as a parable for explaining the Kingdom of Heaven.[13] He gave it precedence by working the first miracle at a marriage feast by request of his mother. Jesus obeyed his mother throughout childhood. He honored her when he declared that she was not only to be esteemed because she bore him in her womb, but because she had kept the word of God perfectly.[14]

At the one and only Sacrifice of Christ on the cross, of which the Eucharistic celebration is a perpetuation through time, it was women, not men who remained faithful and close to the cross, while the apostles fled with the exception of the youngest, John. How is it that now women are excluded from the close vicinity to the altar, while men alone may officiate at close quarters?

Are we really to suppose that these women who accompanied Jesus round Galilee, who looked after him and the apostles, and who were present until the last moment at the foot of the cross, were not present at the Last Supper—the feast of Passover—just because no direct mention is made of them? We have seen that women were not counted at the miracle of the multiplication of the loaves by three out of the four Evangelists. Women and children are normally present at every Passover feast. The Evangelists did not need to mention it. It would go without saying for in every Jewish family it was a common thing.

Women have a specific place in the liturgical observance of Passover given in Haggadah.[15] Women prepare the food according to precise recipes of symbolical implication. It is traditional for women to conduct a search by candlelight in all the corners of the house and to sweep any dust or crumbs with a feather into a wooden spoon, as part of the ritual. Mother and father sit at opposite ends of the table; members of the family and sons and daughters sit on either side. Traditional questions are asked by the children; an explanation is given for the whole family to understand.

Some commentators, to get out of certain difficulties regarding the date of the celebration of Passover at the time of the Passion, have suggested that the Last Supper was not a Passover feast, which would also have done away with the necessary presence of women. Against this argument there is the clear injunction of Jesus to his disciples to prepare the Passover meal. The question of the date can be settled by the tradition that in Galilee the Passover was kept a day earlier than in Judea. There is another reason for concluding that the Last Supper was a Passover meal, for in the account of Luke [16] there is a reference to two chalices. The only satisfactory way of explaining this duplication is to relate it to the traditional four chalices of wine in the Passover ritual. After the third cup of wine called the eucharist, meaning "thanksgiving," and before the fourth cup, the Mazzah or unleavened bread was brought in and handed to the father; he broke it into portions and handed it to each person present. Surely we can see in the ritual a preconceived moment for the institution of the Eucharistic celebration. The Last Supper can therefore have taken place at a Passover meal, and as such women would normally have been present whether they are mentioned or not.

The last thought of Our Lord on the Cross was for his mother. He gave her John as an adopted son, and henceforth all adopted sons of God have Mary as their mother.

CONCLUSION

The Evangelists, true to the custom of their time, did not consider the intellectual opinion of women to be of importance. Such was not the attitude of Jesus Christ himself. He did not fear to shock his disciples by talking to the Samaritan woman. He chose to reveal the most fundamental truths to women. Women accompanied him around the towns and villages in his missionary work. He insisted on women having a new status in married life. He liberated them from certain injustices, such as the stoning of women taken in adultery while men went free. It was women who remained most faithful to him in his Passion, and it was to women that Jesus first appeared after his Resurrection.

The last act that Jesus did on the Cross was to give us his mother through John to be the mother of all. His praise of his mother was not only that she had carried him in her womb, but that she kept the word of God.

IN DEFENSE
OF SAINT PAUL

S<small>AINT</small> P<small>AUL</small> <small>IS GENERALLY CONSIDERED</small> to be an antifeminist. Yet there are very many texts that show he recognized the importance of women's role within the Church. This is clear even before his conversion, for when he made his way into house after house of the new Christian sect, he carried away women as well as men and committed them to prison, which shows he realized that they were active in the propagation of the new faith and hence dangerous.[1] It is surprising that he considered it necessary, because women were not held responsible in Hebrew worship. So he understood that in the Christian faith women had a different role from that held in the Jewish faith.

When Paul became a Christian he continued to rely on women in his missionary work. We hear that when Paul and Silas reached Philippi (a Roman colony and principal city of the district of Macedonia), on the first Sabbath day they went along the river outside the gates to a customary place of prayer. Paul and Silas then sat down and preached to the *women* who had come to the meeting.[2] Here again it is surprising that women are singled out as the first group to whom to speak in the missionary center in Philippi. Hebrews did not consider the teaching of religion to women of great importance, except within the home. Saint Paul did not follow the usual Jewish attitude toward women.

Some of the women at Philippi came from a distance. One of these women, Lydia, came from the town of Thyatira.[3] She was in the purple-dye trade and was evidently a woman of some wealth. After her conversion to Christianity through the preaching of Paul and Silas, she turned her house into a center for the apostles and the faithful. On one occasion, we are told,[4] after Paul and Silas had been liberated from a prison at Philippi, they went immediately to the house of Lydia and met all the brethren there.

This gives some idea of the activity of women in promoting early Christianity gratefully accepted by Paul. It was a common practice for early Christian communities to be established in the houses of women.[5]

There were other towns where the number of women converts was outstanding. At Thessalonika among the Greek converts there were many rich women [6] who joined Paul and Silas. At Borea [7] it is women who are mentioned first among the Gentile converts: "Many Jews became believers, and so did many Greek women from the upper classes and a number of the men."

It is in the long lists of persons to whom Paul sends greetings at the end of his epistles that we see how many women were in the forefront in the service of the early Church and accepted and admired by Paul.

First among the women Paul refers to in his epistles is Phoebe,[8] "our sister, who is in the ministry of the church, that is at Cenchrae." The Douay translation here is more correct than the Jerusalem Bible, which translates the passage as "Phoebe, a deaconess of the church at Cenchrae." The Latin reads: *Commendo autem vobis Phoeben* [*Phoebem* in some manuscripts] *sororem nostram quae est in ministerio ecclesiae, quae est in Cenchris.* In the Greek, the word *ministry* is *diakonon.* It does not necessarily mean that Phoebe was a deaconess, she could have been serving in a higher or lower capacity. Origen (185–254), writing in the early third century, says that in the passage on Phoebe, apostolic authority is given for the constitution of women ministers in the Church.[9]

According to John Chrysostom, in his commentary on the Epistle to the Romans, the reference to Phoebe is taken to mean that Paul accepted her as an ordained deaconess. In his homily 30,[10] he says: "See how many ways he (Paul) takes to give her (Phoebe) dignity. For he has both mentioned her before all others and called her sister. And it is no mean thing to be called sister by Saint Paul. Moreover he has added her *rank* by mentioning her as being a deaconess." And a little later in the same homily he says: "And of the women, one (Phoebe) he addresses by her *title*, for he does not call her servant of the church in an undefined way, because if this were so he would have given Tryphaena and Persis this name too—but one has the *office* of *deaconess*, another as helper and assistant."

Following the passage regarding Phoebe, Saint Paul sends his greetings to Prisca and Aquila, fellow workers in Jesus Christ who had risked their lives for him.[11] We have here a married couple both in the service of the Church. It is to be noted that Paul put the name of the wife, Prisca (Priscilla in some manuscripts, the diminutive of Prisca) first, and the husband's name second. Paul does this on several other occasions when speaking of Prisca, so that probably she was the more active apostle of the two. Paul also greets all the churches of the Gentiles and their own church house.

There are many other references to Priscilla and Aquila in the Acts of the Apostles and in the Epistles of Saint Paul, so that there is a considerable amount of information about them. They had a church-house in Rome on the Aventine Hill. They are believed to have been baptized there by Saint Peter. They left Rome due to the edict of Claudius by which all Jews were expelled from Rome.[12] They then settled in Corinth, where as in Rome they had their own church house.[13] That is where Paul met them for the first time, stayed with them, and worked with them as tentmakers. Paul preached among the Corinthians for eighteen months and moved to Ephesus when the Jews stirred up trouble.[14] Priscilla and Aquila went with him. They stayed at Ephesus, while Saint Paul went on.[15]

It was while Priscilla and Aquila were at Ephesus that Apollos, an intellectual of the Alexandrian Jewish community, arrived in the city and spoke in the synagogue.[16]

Priscilla and Aquila invited Apollos to their house and gave him instruction in the Christian way of life. He became an important apostle. In these accounts the name of Priscilla is constantly put first, and she is looked upon by Saint John Chrysostom and others as having been the principle influence in the conversion of Apollos. She must therefore have been herself a highly educated person. There are scholars who hold that she is the author of the Epistle to the Hebrews,[17] the only unsigned epistle attributed to Saint Paul. When the Jewish persecution in Italy ceased, Priscilla and Aquila returned to Rome and continued to hold their house as an ecclesiastical center. There is a mention of their church-house in a Vatican codex.[18]

It would be ludicrous to imagine that Paul would ever have suggested that Priscilla should consult her husband at home on questions of religion as in the well-known passage in the First Epistle to the Corinthians regarding women being silent in churches (I Corinthians 14:34–35). In a number of Greek and Old Latin manuscripts these verses appear only at the end of the chapter as verses 39 and 40.[19] The fact that these verses get moved about makes them a likely interpolation. Among the codices in which this transposition takes place is the Claramontanus Codex of the sixth century,[20] both in the Greek and Latin texts, and in the Latin Armagh Codex of the ninth century.[21]

The Old Latin versions were prior to the Latin of the Vulgate. It was especially in the earliest period of the text that interpolations could be introduced. At that time the books of the New Testament had not come to be regarded as on the level of the Old Testament. In the Old Latin versions, verse 36 of I Corinthians 14 of the Vulgate came after verse 33, so that the verse *An a vobis Sermo Dei processit* (Does the Word of God proceed from you, does it reach you alone?) applied then to the prophets in general. In the Vulgate it applies to women prophets only. When one remembers the deference in which Paul spoke of his fellow workers, both male and female, one wonders if this awkward phrase could really be that of Saint Paul at all. It sounds more like a marginal note of an irritated scribe. The injunction in verse 35 of the Vulgate and 40 of the Old Latin versions telling wives to consult their husbands at home, might have been possible by the end of the second century when there would have been a sufficient number of Christian married couples, but at the time of Saint Paul there would have been very few. Paul could not have told Lois the fervent Christian grandmother of Timothy nor his Christian mother Eurice to consult their husbands, since those men were pagans.

Paul taught that Christian wives could continue to live with their pagan husbands if the husband consented. It was thought that the wife's spirit of obedience would win over the husband. This obedience did not entail her religious belief. Both Peter and Paul required obedience of the wife to the husband as the slave to his master. The apostles were in no position to change the whole social system.

The passage that commands men to worship with their heads uncovered and women with veils [22] is also surprising, if dated back to the time of Paul himself, for Jewish men worshiped with their heads covered and still do. Greek women did not usually wear veils indoors. They wore them out-of-doors to indicate that they were lawfully married and not harlots. If harlots wore a veil they were punished for doing so.

Whatever arguments are brought forward to prove that in Saint Paul's teaching women held a secondary place to men are wiped out by the very clear statement that all who are baptized in Christ are clothed in Christ, and that there is no distinction between Jew and Greek, slave and free, male and female, and that we are all one in Christ.[23] We are all sons of God and we are all spouses of Christ whether we are men or women. If only men may represent Christ, then only women may represent the Church, the Spouse of Christ. These allegorical analogies do not make sense if carried too far.

The passage in Galatians regarding no discrimination between the sexes is well known. Few know that a similar passage comes in the Epistle to the Colossians in some Greek and Old Latin manuscripts.[24] It is particularly interesting because it comes after a reference to creation in Genesis and that by baptism (the putting off of the old man and the putting on of the new) mankind as the image of God is renewed, "where there is neither male nor female, Gentile nor Jew, circumcised nor non-circumcised, barbarian nor Scythian, slave nor freeman."

The passage from Galations referring to no discrimination of the sexes comes at the end of the list of the persons not to be discriminated against. In the passage of Colossians of the Old Latin versions, no discrimination between the sexes is placed first on the list. Both passages in the Vulgate and in the Old Latin versions are in contradiction to the interpretation given in I Corinthian 11:7, where men are said to be made in the image of God, but women only as the glory of man.

The number of manuscripts and quotations from the writings of the Fathers that show the reference to male and female at the beginning of the list is very considerable. Besides the Claramontanus Codex and the Armagh, there are the writings of Ambrose, Augustine, Jerome, Sedulius Hibernius, and the Borner Greek Codex, the Codex Regius I, and Sangermanensis.[25]

So there is no doubt that Saint Paul Epistles have suffered by interpolations and in particular in passages regarding women, which can be considered the work of antifeminist scribes.

Among the English translations, for example, the Jerusalem Bible, we would expect that in the full and lengthy notes that accompany nearly every verse, reference would be made to the Old Latin versions in the passage regarding no discrimination of sexes in Colossians 3. A note draws attention to the fact that some versions add the word *amen* to the same passage, which is an interesting point because it means that probably it was part of a liturgical text, perhaps a baptismal service. But the editor has made no mention of the variation in the Old Latin texts regarding the addition of "male and female" left out in the Vulgate and yet used by Jerome himself in his own writings.

Saint Paul has been maligned; he has been made to appear to hold opinions he did not have. The truth will not remain hidden forever.

APPENDIX IV

EMPRESSES AND QUEENS
WITH POWERS OF
REX ET SACERDOS

THE STATUS OF WOMEN in the Byzantine court was very high. Nowhere is it clearer that Christianity had been at first beneficial to the position of women. Byzantium was a Greek-speaking country, but there was nothing left of the ancient Greek's disdain of women. The Byzantine empresses were participants in the social and political activities of the country. Roman empresses it is true had had some political power but not to the extent enjoyed by the Byzantine empresses. Nor did the Macedonian queens have the same equality. The Egyptian queens did, but they had had it for centuries without influencing Greece.

There were many outstanding Byzantine empresses, highly cultured and capable rulers. They were corulers [1] with emperors, often regents for their sons or younger brothers, and on some occasion rulers in their own right. The Empress Pulcheria governed as regent for her brother Theodosius II during his minority and was influential throughout his reign. After his death she reigned in her own right; Marcian became coruler with her on the understanding that the marriage would not be consummated. Although decrees were issued in both their names, there is no doubt that in religious matters Pulcheria was the driving power;

this is attested by the letters of Pope Leo the Great.[2] Pulcheria was present at the Church Councils held during her reign.

Theodora, the wife of Justinian, ruled with him. The oaths of allegiance were taken to her as well as to him.[3] Zonarus, the historian, held that Theodora was no less powerful than Justinian in matters of government. He considered that both should be praised for the reformation of the law code. He saw the influence of Theodora especially in the *Novellae* 85, 128, 134, and 161.[4] Both Justinian and Theodora promoted the building of churches; Theodora in particular founded hospitals.

The Empress Irene, wife of Leo IV, was regent for her son Constantine VI during his minority. Later she reigned in her own right. Her most outstanding contribution was her part in the seventh General Council. The empresses as regents took over all the same duties and rights of the emperor. The emperors considered themselves to be *basileus* (king) and *hieros* (priest). They had the duty to govern the empire in religious matters as well as in political affairs. The Empress Irene exercised the same power as an emperor when she convoked the seventh General Council. All the first eight General Councils were convoked by emperors or empresses.

When Leo IV died in 780 he left Irene as sole guardian for her son. She ruled for ten years as regent and displayed great firmness and audacity during a period of great unrest due to the Iconoclastic controversy, the movement against the use of sculptured and painted images in worship. Monks and people were in favor of the visual arts; the military and some members of the episcopate were against it.

The preceding emperors had been iconoclastic; but no sooner had Irene been recognized as empress than she began to work with prudent moderation for the reestablishment of the use of images; one step was to call back the monks who had been expelled. She elected Tarasius, a person on her side, as patriarch. After a period of six years she decided on the necessity of a General Council of the Church to settle the matter and bring peace to her kingdom. Irene convoked all archbishops and bishops of the East, and she sent an invitation to Pope Adrian I. The pope replied by a letter that was read in the council, and he sent two legates to represent him. The first assembly was interrupted by the military.[5] Undaunted, Irene dispatched the military to a northern region and then disbanded them. A year later she reconvoked the council. The first seven sessions were held at Nicaea, and the final session in Constantinople. The assembly opened on September 24, 787, with 367 bishops present,[6] and the two legates from Rome. An address of the empress was read at the first session. She was undoubtedly present at all the sessions, for a formal acclamation was made at the end of each session wishing the empress and emperor and all present a long life, in which Irene was referred to as a "New Helen"[7] and her son a "New Constantine." The reason for this reference to a "New Helen" is explained by a letter of Pope Adrian I to Charlemagne, in reply to his objections to Irene's address read at the seventh General Council. Adrian justifies Irene's address and participation in the council on the grounds that Helen, the mother of Constantine, sat in a synod at Rome together with her son and in the presence of Pope Sylvester, at which judgement was passed on a matter brought up by the Jews. Pope Adrian further strengthened his argument by reference to the letter of Pope Leo I to Pulcheria who likewise sat in her own right to the fourth General Council.

On another occasion Pope Gregory the Great wrote to the Empress Leontia recommending her to follow the example of Pulcheria, who in the Holy Synod was called a "New Helen."[8] So we see that whenever a person is called a "New Helen" it is due to her having taken part at a Church Council. Bishop Turgot, the earliest biographer of Saint Margaret of Scotland, likewise justifies her participation in the Church Councils of Scotland, which she herself had convoked, on the grounds that Margaret was a "New Helen" following the example of the mother of Constantine.[9]

According to the continuator of the Chronicles of Theophanes,[10] Irene and Constantine VI were present at the last session of the seventh General Council held in Constantinople at the Magnauram Palace, where the decrees of the council were read and signed by the young emperor and Irene and all the bishops. There followed a procession to the Basilica of Hagia Sophia where the Cross was again displayed publicly and a solemn liturgy celebrated. A memorandum of the council, written in a letter from Photius to Michael of Bulgaria, describes how the 367 bishops took their place in the Basilica. The emperor and empress are said to have donned their purple robes of state and that together with the bishops, acting in their own right, they officially condemned the Iconoclastic heresy.[11]

The empresses of the Ottonian period of the Holy Roman Empire can be compared to the Byzantine empresses for their culture and political enterprise and status within the Church. Edith (Edgitha), the English-born princess, sister of King Aethelsten, was given the city of Magdeburg as her "Morning Gift" on her marriage to Otto I.[12] The city became the outstanding archbishopric of Germany. The practice of placing whole cities under the direction of a woman was likewise repeated by Otto I when he made his daughter Matilda abbess and governor of the whole town of Quedlinburg.[13] Her brother Otto II created her *Matrix* for all Saxony. Adelheid, the second wife of Otto I, was *Statthalterin* of Pavia.[14] By Otto II's marriage to the Byzantine princess Theophanu the traditions of the Byzantine Empire were carried through to the West.

Queen Margaret of Scotland likewise brought the traditions of the Byzantine Empire from her native Hungary to Scotland. She was only about nine years old when she left Hungary for England, but in those times a child of nine was nearly mature. Margaret was to play an even greater part in the Scottish Church Councils than did the Byzantine Empress Irene in the seventh General Council, for Margaret not only convoked and presided at the Church Synods but she was also the chief speaker in the discussions and chief promoter in the liturgical reforms.[15]

After living in the court of King Edward the Confessor, her uncle, in 1066 she fled to Scotland when William the Conqueror usurped the throne of England. She was married to King Malcolm. Bishop Turgot, her confessor, tells us that Margaret observed that the liturgical practices used at that time in Scotland were not the same as those used by the universal Church. As queen she was able to arrange for several synods to correct these differences. The most important of these synods, according to

Turgot, was the one that lasted three days, during which Margaret with only a few people on her side held an open discussion with a large number of dissenting clergy who spoke in defense of their customs. Margaret, by her knowledge of the Scriptures, was able to persuade the clergy to conform with the rites of the universal Church.

At the synods, King Malcolm acted as Margaret's interpreter, for although he did not know how to read, for he was a warrior and mainly occupied in fighting, he did know Celtic, a language unknown to Margaret. Margaret's main arguments were:

1. Those who served God in one faith ought to use the customary universal rites and not practice other farfetched usages.

2. The fast for Lent should start on Ash Wednesday and not on the Monday after the first Sunday of Lent. The Scottish clergy objected as they believed that Jesus fasted six weeks. Margaret pointed out that the number of days mentioned in the Gospels was forty. The point was accepted, and from that time Lent was kept from Ash Wednesday.

3. It was wrong to neglect receiving the Body and Blood of Christ on the festival of Easter. The clergy defended themselves on the ground that it was for fear of eating and drinking unworthily that they refrained following the warning of Saint Paul and knowing themselves to be sinners. Margaret maintained that the meaning of the passage did not require all to withhold from Communion, because if so, the words of Christ would be contradicted: "except you shall eat of the flesh of the son of Man and drink his Blood, you shall not have life in you." Furthermore, she explained that Saint Paul was speaking about those who do not discern the Body of the Lord and do not distinguish the Sacraments from bodily food. And she added, we, who have previously made confession of our sins and have been cleansed by penance and fasts and almsgiving, can approach our Lord's table on the feast of the Resurrection as a health-giving preparation for eternal happiness.

4. Certain practices used in the celebration of Mass by Scottish clergy she pointed out were contrary to universal usage. Margaret, by her holiness and knowledge of the Scriptures, was able to persuade the clergy to discontinue these practices.

5. The Lord's day—Sunday—should be distinguished from all other days, following the custom practiced since the time of Gregory the Great.

6. Certain contracts of marriage were unlawful, such as the marriage of a man to his stepmother, or a man to the widow of his deceased brother.

The Celtic clergy were finally convinced by Margaret's arguments and agreed to adopt all proposals.

It is important to the thesis of this book to note that at the time that Bishop Turgot wrote his biography of the queen, it was thought very commendable that she should have undertaken the task of convoking the Church Synods. Her interventions were warmly approved by Lanfranc, the Archbishop of Canterbury. He sent her a laudatory letter in reply to her invitation to him requesting his presence at the synods.[16] He complied by sending Godwin as his legate. It was Margaret's ardor in upholding the universal Church practices that led to her canonization.[17]

The work of Margaret shows there has been a tradition in the Church of women holding administrative positions. The empresses and the queens by the sacrament of their crowning were considered to hold certain sacerdotal powers, although they were never ordained to celebrate the Eucharist.

Elizabeth I of England, as Supreme Governor of the Church of England, was considered to have the right to rule over both spiritual and temporal matters according to the oath of 1559 taken by the clergy.[18] Similar oaths were made by canons and clergy to the abbesses with quasi-episcopal jurisdiction in their "separated" territories. John Jewel in his *Apology of the Church of England*, written in 1562,[19] asserted the right of sovereignty to rule the religious establishments in their realms, based on the fact that the four General Councils of the Church were convoked by the emperors and empresses.

Today the oaths of a bishop to Her Majesty, the Queen of England, still acknowledge her spiritual and temporal jurisdiction.[20] They still place their hands in her hands when they make the act of homage.

THE ORDINATION
OF ABBESSES

THE WORD *ordained* is used for the consecration of an abbess in several sacramentaries. In the Mozarabic *Liber Ordinum*, Chapter 23 is entitled *Ordo Ad Ordinandum Abbatissam*.[1] The instructions require that when an abbess is ordained she is to be clothed as *Deo votis* in sacred religious vestments and crowned with a miter. At the altar the bishop is to invest her with a pallium and say the following prayer:

Omnipotens Domine Deus, apud quem non est discretio sexuum, nec ulla sanctarum disparilitas animarum, qui ita viro ad spiritalia certamina corrobas.

So we have here a very clear statement that before God there is no discrimination of sex, and that women in the same way as men are called to collaborate in the spiritual struggle. This sacramentary was used from the fifth to the eleventh centuries.

In the sacramentary of the Moisac Monastery the ordination rite for abbesses is the same as for abbots.[2] They are to be clothed with the alb, and a stole is to be put about their necks. The abbots or abbesses are then required to prostrate themselves before the altar. In the prayer the tradition is carried back to the sister of Moses, Miriam.

The priestly and episcopal insignia that was presented to the abbesses are proof of their earlier clerical status.

The alb, or rochet, is a liturgical garment worn by clergy over a secular dress when officiating. The stole is the band of silk or other material that is worn by deacons over the shoulder. The other insignia given to the abbess are directly indicative of a pastoral and episcopal office; that is, the crozier, the pectoral cross, the ring, gloves, and miter.

Sister Telchilde O.S.B., a member of the Benedictine Order now established at Jouarre, has collected interesting information regarding the croziers and other episcopal insignia found in the tombs of the past abbesses.[3] In 1543, at the entombment of the Abbess Madeleine d'Orléans, a nun walked in procession carrying on a sheep skin the abbess's crozier, which was buried with her.[4] When in 1861 the tomb of the Abbess Louise de Bourbon, who died in 1586, was opened, her episcopal ring was found; it contained a precious inset diamond.[5] In 1627 the tomb of the seventh-century bishop Ebregisile—brother of the first abbess—was opened, there was found his episcopal ring, which has been worn by the abbesses of the Abbey of Jouarre ever since. In a manuscript describing the entombment of the Abbess Jeanne de Bourbon, she is said to have been buried with her veil and crown, her episcopal ring and gloves by her side. These examples show a long and continuous tradition of the episcopal insignia worn by the abbesses.

The term *sacerdos* has been applied to women as well as to men. It is not possible to hold, as some writers have done, that women *sacerdotes* were just wives of priests. The following examples give ample proof to the contrary.

At the Cathedral of Saint John the Baptist in Monza, there was a mixed choir of men and women *sacerdotes* from a double monastery who were obliged to officiate in the chanting of Divine Office day and night.[6] The Cathedral dates from the sixth century.

There is a reference to men and women *sacerdotes* in the tenth-century Saxon Chronicle by the historian Widukind, a Benedictine monk of the Monastery of Corvey in Germany.[7] He mentions a terrible storm that took place in his own lifetime. He says that priests of both sexes (*utriusque sexus sacerdotes*) were struck by lightning and that many churches were hit. In the several early manuscripts that exist of Widukind's book, which include the phrase *utriusque sexus sacerdotes*, one later twelfth-century manuscript changes the word *sexus* to *ordinis: utriusque ordinis sacerdotes*.[8]

Paul Hirsch, in his German translation of the text,[9] leaves out the line regarding priests of both sexes: *utriusque sexus sacerdotes*, and in a footnote interprets the phrase as meaning that "men and women called out; priests were hit by lightning."[10] This is a deliberate hiding of the truth. Such an interpretation is certainly not possible of the text in codex Steinfeld[11] in the British Museum, which I have consulted myself. The words *sexus sacerdotes* are written so closely together as to form one word and leaves no room for a possible semicolon. There is no doubt that Hirsch understood the real meaning, because in his Latin publication of the Widukind Chronicle, he has carefully listed all the manuscripts containing the line *utriusque sexus sacerdotes*.[12]

As already mentioned, the twelfth-century Codex Sigelberti uses the phrase *utriusque ordinis sacerdotes* in place of *utriusque sexus sacerdotes*, and this gives us a clue that these ordained men and women may have belonged to canonical or religious orders such as Quedlinburg, Herford, Gandersheim, and the many Canoness Institutes, which were either double monasteries or women's abbeys with a group of canons attached.

Such a supposition is fully borne out by the Saxon chronicles of George Fabricius[13] in which he mentions the ordination of abbesses and nuns to the office of *Sacerdos Maxima* or *Sacerdos*, listing some twenty or more well-known women.

George Fabricius was a Lutheran writer of the sixteenth century, a professor of Latin and Greek, a German historian who conscientiously researched early Latin documents as became the fashion at the time of the Renaissance, and in particular at the time of the Reformation, by members of the Reformed Churches who sought to justify their doctrines as being based on primitive custom. Fabricius makes no comment on his finding of women *sacerdotes*. He may not have been very interested in the fact, but he notes it diligently as a historian.

Fabricius was born in 1516.[14] His parents, George Goldschmid and Margaret née Pisonis, looked after their children's education with every care. Many of Fabricius' letters were addressed to his brothers, Blasius, Jacobus, and Andrew. There are no letters addressed to his sisters; he does not seem to have had any particular profeminist leanings. After completing his academic studies at Leipzig, he spent four years in Italy, where he made friends with erudite scholars. He adopted the Latinized name of Fabricius, a not unusual device at that time. He was a serious scholar fired by the new learning of the Renaissance and inspired by the golden age of the Greek and Latin poets. On his return to Germany he felt called to the Lutheran ministry and became rector of a school at Abrani, Saxony. He was a dedicated professor and produced Latin and Greek grammars for his students. He wrote a commentary on Genesis and on the Gospels, and collected historical documents on his native Saxony. He produced four volumes of historical research: *Originum Saxonicarum, Germania Magna, Praecipue Saxonia Memorabilium,* and *Rerum Misnicarum.* He also wrote poems in Latin and composed music for them. He edited works of early Christian writers before it became a common thing; these included the works of Aurelius Prudentius, Tertullian, Cyprian, Ambrose, and Fortunatus.

It is inconceivable that a scholarly writer of this stature should invent the title of *Sacerdos Maxima* and apply it to abbesses without reliable sources on historical grounds. He had no reason to do so. He does not comment on the fact but just noted them down in the text and the index. Fabricius gave the annals of Quedlinburg as being one of his sources. The original manuscript was at Dresden, but since the war is no longer to be found, and presumed lost.

In Liber I, p. 27 of *Originum Saxonicarum* there is a reference to four Anglo-Saxon abbesses, well known to us through Bede, who are each said by Fabricius to have been made *Sacerdos Maxima.* Edelfrida [15] by consent of her husband was made *Sacerdos Maxima* in the community founded by Ebba. In the index of the book *Originum Saxonicarum* Ebba is likewise listed as a *Sacerdos Maxima,* although she is not mentioned in the text. Fabricius mentions Edelberga as having been created *Sacerdos Maxima* of Brigg: *Adelberga creatur Sacerdos Maxima Brigensis;* [16] and Serburga (Sexburga), who after the death of her husband Erconberto, joined her eldest sister, Etheldreda, at Ely, remained a widow, and soon succeeded to Etheldreda in *dignitate Ecclesiastica*.[17] This corresponds to the same account in Bede and in the *Liber Eliensis*. Christina, daughter of King Edmund and sister of Queen Margaret of Scotland, is said to be a *sacerdos*.[18]

There is no doubt that at this time in England the abbesses of religious orders were considered to have high ecclesiastical office. Hilda and her community took part in the Whitby Synod organized on her own territory.[19] The five abbesses called to a council convened by King Wihtred at Beccanceld, near Sittingbourne, all signed the decrees issued, after the name of the archbishop but before all other clergy.[20] At the Synod of Nidd, Aelfrida, who succeeded to Hilda as Abbess of Whitby, is called *consiliatrix* of the whole province and was one of the main speakers during the debate.[21]

Fabricius refers to many German women of religious institutes and orders with the title of *Sacerdos, Sacerdos Maxima,* or *virgines Sacerdotes*.

At Gandersheim the well-known writer Roswitha is said to be a *Sacerdos*,[22] not a *Sacerdos Maxima*. This is understandable because Roswitha herself was not abbess, but subject to the Abbess Geberga I. Fabricius mentions that *Roswitha Sacerdos* wrote prose and hymns and a panegyric on Otto I. When Fabricius mentions Geberga II, the Abbess of Gandershiem, daughter of Henry the Duke of Bavaria and of Judith von Bayern, he still refers to her as *Sacerdos*[23] and not *Sacerdos Maxima*, which is surprising. Fabricius' use of that title may have been because Gandersheim was at one time dependent on Quedlinburg, and the abbess might perhaps not have the position of a *Sacerdos Maxima*. Geberga's sister Helica was likewise *Sacerdos Pataviensem*,[24] not *Maxima*. Sophia, the daughter of Queen Gisela of Hungary, is said to be *Sacerdos Maxima*[25] of Paderborn. Sophia, the daughter of Ditericus and his Polish wife Dobrogneva, in Germany called Liutgardi, was a *Sacerdos Gebstebten*.[26] The third daughter of Adela and Premislao of Bohemia was made a *Sacerdos Maxima Gerenrhoden*.[27] Adelheid and Hedwig, daughters of Henry I of Thuringia, are called *virgines Sacerdotes Vueisenuelsi*.[28] It would seem, therefore, that widows could also be *sacerdotes* as otherwise there would be no need to specify that these *sacerdotes* were virgins. Certainly when the word *maxima* is attached it signifies that the *Sacerdos* has a preeminent post either as abbess, or possibly indicates her descent from a royal family, although this did not always follow.

Agnes of Bohemia is said to be *Sacerdos* of Prague.[29] She was daughter of Premysil Ottocar I, King of Bohemia, and of Constantia,[30] the sister of King Andreas of Hungary. Her brother Wenceslaus IV succeeded to the throne of Bohemia in 1230. Fabricius mistakenly calls Agnes the daughter of Wenceslaus. There are several letters extant between Agnes and Gregory IX, who esteemed her very highly and held her up as an example to be followed together with Saint Elizabeth, when he wrote to Beatrix, Queen of Castile.[31] She was requested in marriage by the Emperor of the Holy Roman Empire Frederick II and by King Henry III of England, both of whom she refused so that she might dedicate her life to the Order of Saint Clare. Agnes was abbess of the Order of Saint Clare, then called Saint Damian. She was a contemporary of Saint Clare, and both persisted in their demand for the privilege of absolute poverty; that is, the right to have no possessions at all.

Agnes was installed as abbess in Prague in 1234, but the Rule of Saint Benedict was imposed on the community, which entailed holding possessions and receiving revenues from the Hospital of Prague, which by spirit of poverty according to the rule of Saint Francis they did not want. In 1243 Innocent IV permitted them their own way of life. Wadding, in his writings on the *Annales Minorem*, in lauding Agnes says: *"quod cum unctio Sancti Spiritis docuerit Agnetem"* [32] suggesting she was consecrated with holy oil, as *Sacerdos* and abbess.

Three abbesses of Quedlinburg are said to have been called *Sacerdos Maxima*; Adelheid,[33] the sister of Henry Fowler, according to Kettner's interpretation of the passage in Fabricius (the source used by Fabricius is given as *Origines et Chronicum Brunsuigium*; Matilda,[34] the daughter of the builder of the monastery (whom we know was Otto I, but whom Fabricius considered as Henry Fowler); and Sophia, "the strong and prudent woman," who in 1203 was made the third *Sacerdos Maxima* of Quedlinburg and who, Fabricius mentions, was later deprived of her dignity, by which, we understand, she was excommunicated by reason of her refusal to accommodate the Palm Sunday procession pilgrims, already referred to earlier, but was reinstated by Innocent III.[35]

The latest date mentioned by Fabricius in reference to a *Sacerdota Maxima* is Beatrix, *Magnam Sacerdotem Suselicensum*,[36] who lived to an exceptional old age and died in 1310.

The hierarchical status of the abbesses in Quedlinburg can be judged by the accounts of the consecration of the abbesses. The Abbess Mechtild was consecrated in the Cathedral of Halberstadt in the presence of some twelve archbishops and bishops.[37]

The titles given to canonesses as witnesses of documents issued by abbesses of Quedlinburg are also illuminating, the hierarchical position of the canonesses in Quedlinburg corresponding with the position of the canons who were under the abbesses.

In the time of Adelheid de Curte Salta, in the reign of Henry IV, a diploma was signed in 1068 in the presence of the sisters and brothers and ministers of the churches.[38] The women witnesses are named first: Evezza *praeposita* and Cilica *Decana;* and then the men: Frederick *Custos*, Tiodo *Pr.*, and Himo *Laicus*, and Frederick.

In the time of Abbess Gertrude, a document dated 1241 was signed in the presence of the following witnesses: *Machtildis, Ecclesiae nostrae Praeposita, Ricza Decana, Mactildis Minorum Praeposita, Sophia Custos et coeterae nostrae canonicae.* There follows the list of the men witnesses: *Conradus Ecclesiae sancti Wiperti Praepositus, Fredericus Prior, Sigfridus Quenstede, Johannes Leo Arnoldus Custos et Hermannus noster Notarius, reliqui canonici nostri.*[39]

In Milan in 1115, a priest named Azo was called *Praepositus et primicerius lectorum;* he belonged to the second group of *decumani* of Saint Tecla's. It has been sustained that in earlier centuries the *decumani* of the second group would probably have been canonesses.[40]

In the hierarchical order of the witnesses at Quedlinburg, the *Praeposita* is given first place, before the *Decana*, the *Minor Decana*, and the *Custos*. And in the list of canons, the *Praepositus* of the Church of Saint Wilpert was placed before the prior. There was no abbot because at that time the abbess was head of the men's order of canons. The canons of Saint Wilpert were not made independent of the abbess of Quedlinburg until 1265 when the abbess renounced her rights to Saint Wilpert by a letter.[41]

In Monza, Italy, there was likewise a *custos* who was a priest. *Vicentius venerabilis Archipresbiter,*[42] *et Custos Ecclesie e Canonice beati Xti. Martyris Sancti Johannis.* That is he was *custos* of the Cathedral of Saint John the Baptist in Monza. It is evident that the names *praepositus* and *custos* were normally given to ordained persons, and therefore the *praeposita* and the *custos* of the canonesses of Quedlinburg would have been ordained persons, although they are not likely to have been Mass-saying priests due to the tradition against women in their monthly periods touching the Blessed Sacrament. And likewise the term *Sacerdos* used by Fabricius would have been given to the ordained canonesses, though probably not Mass-saying priests.

In Rome at the monastery of the sanctimoniales of Saint Cyriacus [43] there were similar titles: *Praeposita, magistra, priorissa, diaconissa, rectrix, custrix,* and so on.

There is a tradition that Saint Brigid of Kildare was ordained a bishop. This generally is considered just a legend by prejudiced writers who are not acquainted with the quasi-episcopal status of abbesses, which make the legend very much more likely. Legends sometimes turn out to be historical facts. Saint Patrick is said to have practiced the penitential form of prayer of 350 genuflections daily. I used to think this a pious exaggeration until I visited the Convent of the Orthodox Coptic Nuns of Abu Sefan in Cairo and found that the nuns today perform the 350 genuflections daily and that these have to be completed by noon.

According to the oldest account of the life of Saint Brigid, by Cogitosus,[44] and also the "Nicar Brigit" hymn, Brigid was consecrated a virgin by Bishop Mac Caille.[45] A later account says that Bishop Mac Caille accompanied Brigid to the Bishop Mel of Mash. He was presumably the same as Mel of Mag Teloch, patron of the diocese of Ardagh, who died in 487 or 488. The story is told that Bishop Mel consecrated Brigid a bishop while drunk.[46] He did not have to be drunk to do so, for the anonymous Irish writer[47] of the seventh century tells us that there was a First and Second Order of Saints, and that the First Order consisted chiefly of bishops, and he adds "women were among their number." The First Order is dated 440–543, which coincides with the date of Saint Brigid, 452–500. The Second Order, dated 543–99, was chiefly composed of priests, but at this time we are told "women had been withdrawn from the administration of the Church and separated into monasteries apart from men."

What was the position of these women bishops? There is a passage in the life of Saint Brigid by Cogitosus that suggests that she had the jurisdiction of a bishop like the European abbesses, but possibly not sacerdotal, for she is said to have called "a great man from his solitary life to govern the church with her in episcopal dignity so that nothing of the sacerdotal order should be wanting in her churches, nor in the churches of her province."

Brigid evidently did not have sacerdotal ordination, although ordained a bishop, for otherwise she would not have been required to call in another person.

Brigid is said to have preached to the people. People of both sexes came to devote themselves to her. She had large territories and held churches within these territories. So we can look upon her as an *Episcopa*, an overseer of churches and people in the same way as in early Christian times in the East and in the West.

Brigid's successors were likewise entitled to receive episcopal orders.[48]

CONCLUSION

We can conclude that women from earliest times were ordained to an administrative position within the Church. They at times received the titles of *Episcopa*, *Sacerdota Maxima*, *Praeposita*, and *Custos* of churches. They had all the powers of a bishop with regard to the jurisdiction of churches and people within their territories. It cannot be concluded, although they were called *sacerdos*, that they were consecrated for the celebration of the Eucharist, at least not until past fifty or sixty years of age. Even if the ordination was the same as that of men, as women they would have of their own accord withheld from touching the Eucharistic species. Although the idea of women's impurity was based on a completely mistaken understanding of genetics, which has been the reason for withholding her from full priestly ordination, it nevertheless stands as witness to the belief in the true presence of Christ in the Blessed Sacrament. It was the fear of contaminating so holy a thing that led to all the precautions, such as staying at a distance from the altar and not going to Communion during menstrual periods, that has brought about restrictions that today no longer make any sense.

ABBESSES WITH POWERS
OF CONFESSION

THERE WERE four rules of religious orders in which the abbess is mentioned as having the duty of hearing confession. These were: the Rule of Saint Columban with the example of Abbess Fara [1] of Brie; the Rule of Saint Donatus; [2] the *Regula Cujusdam ad Virginis;* [3] and the Rule of Saint Basil. [4]

The Rule of Saint Columban required confession to be heard three times a day. In the life of Saint Columban by Jonas, a monk of the order, several accounts are given of the occasions when Fara, the Abbess of Brie, heard confessions. Mabillon justifies her doing this by pointing out that she was following the Eastern tradition. As the Rule of Columban was adopted by many foundations throughout Europe, the custom of frequent confession must have been practiced in many places.

In the Rule of Saint Donatus, both young and senior nuns are exhorted to confess every day at any hour and not to hide anything from the *Matris Spirituale*. They were to confess before meals or after, whenever it was convenient, because, it was added, confession liberated the penitent from death. It is evident that the confession was considered to be sacramental.

The *Regula Cujusdam ad Virginis*, of an unknown women's order, considered prior to the time of Saint Benedict, contained the query whether an abbess had the right to delegate another nun to hear confession in her place. The reply was in the affirmative, but on condition that the nun maintained the seal of silence. She was, however, permitted to report the matter to the abbess.

In the Basilian Rule the question was asked whether a nun should confess to the mother of the monastery or to a priest. The reply given was that it was more honest and devout for the senior mother to be present with the confessor during the nun's confession, so that the mother would know what penance had been imposed for the correction of the sin. It must be remembered that the Rule of Saint Basil is not considered to be the work of Saint Basil nor yet of Saint Macrina, the foundress of the Basilian Order.[5] The fact that the question was asked shows that at one time nuns did confess to the senior mother.

The history of confession shows that there was a very different attitude in early times to that of the present. Old Irish Penitentials, the Penitentials of Theodore of Canterbury and others, give guidance to confessors as to the penances that should be imposed according to the sin committed. Anyone who kills a son or daughter must do penance for twenty years; anyone who kills a brother or sister must do penance for ten years; anyone who kills a father or mother must do penance for fourteen years.[6]

The penalties were of various kinds. They could be abstention from Holy Communion for many years, fasting, singing of psalms, pilgrimages, floggings. Basil, in a letter to Amphilochius, required as a penance for adultery a period of penance for fifteen years, divided into four years with the weepers, five with the hearers, four with the kneelers, and two with the standers, during which the penitent could not go to Communion. Gregory of Nyssa prescribed thirty-six years of penance for homicide, nine in each of the foregoing grades. When contrition was manifest the nine year periods could be shortened to eight, seven, or six years.

Among the Celts the confessor was the soul-friend, in Irish *anmchara*, which may have been derived from *anachoreta*. Anchorites and hermits—that is, people living outstanding holy lives—were looked on as the most desirable confessors. Saint Ita of Cluain Credill, a virgin teacher, is said to have heard confessions.[7]

Saint Brigid advocated the need for everybody to have a soul-friend.[8] The Celtic tradition was carried by Columbanus to his many foundations in Bobbio, Italy, in Bourges, Chelles, Fecamp, Jouarre, Jumieges, Faremoutier, Montvilliers, Nevers, Nivelles, just to mention a few in France and Belgium. It is not, therefore, surprising that abbesses had the right to hear confession.

In the *Capitularium regum Francorum* it was called an abuse that some abbesses were known to give benediction by the imposition of hands on the heads of men.[9] This is understood to mean that they gave absolution to men who had confessed to them. It does not say that it was an abuse for an abbess to impose her hands on the heads of women. Certainly women continued to hear confession.

In 1210 Innocent III withdrew the right of the abbesses of Las Huelgas from hearing confession.[10] By that time it was considered an abuse and therefore must have entailed absolution. It was only at the fourth Latern Council in 1215 that the general law on confession was formed.[11] In 1255 at Poitiers, deacons were forbidden to hear confessions. Priests and deacons had been earlier incorporated into a decree by Gratian, which was continued at the Council of London in 1200, at Rouen in 1231, by Saint Edmund of Canterbury in 1236, and by Walter of Kirkham, Bishop of Durham, in 1255.[12] As there is no doubt that abbesses had the ordination of deaconess or archdeaconess as at Münster,[13] and as the ordination of a deacon was considered at one time sufficient for the hearing of confessions, this may explain how it was that abbesses, such as those at Las Huelgas, considered they had the right to do so.

Besides this, abbesses may have received a sacerdotal ordination as proved in Appendix V. Even if they did not undertake the work of a Mass-saying priest for reasons of ritual impurity,[14] they would not have considered it necessary to refrain from hearing confession.

Later, of course, the ordination of the abbess was lowered to a status of a blessing only. As such, it was denied that she could hold the power of the keys. The diminished status took place slowly, over hundreds of years, so that one generation would not have realized what the position had been in early periods.

Women seem to have been specially apt as spiritual directors. Hilda was the "mother of all"; Aelfleda was the counselor of her district; the abbesses were "spiritual mothers" with a special duty to assist the nuns under their care in their development according to Christian ideals.

DUAL CATHEDRALS AND THEIR SIGNIFICANCE TO WOMEN

UAL CATHEDRALS were to be found both in the East and the West from about the fourth century. The reasons given are that one was for catechumens and the other for the fully initiated. It must be remembered that baptism was often put off to very late in life, and people remained catechumens for a long time. Another possible reason given was the necessary division of sexes at the adult baptisms, when very many people were baptized on one day; that is, on the vigil of Easter or of Pentecost, later also of Christmas. The excavation of the site of the dual cathedral of Trèves of the fourth century suggests this. There were two equally long rectangular churches either side of two baptismal fonts.

In the ninth century, however, there must have been another reason. The second cathedral, in several places, was built at a much later date than the first cathedral; it was smaller and generally dedicated to Our Lady. These were particularly frequent in Lombardy, in Milan,[1] Pavia,[2] Bergamo,[3] Como,[4] and Aqueleia.[5] There were also many in Gaul,[6] Switzerland [7] and in countries on the Rhine.[8]

Many historians have been puzzled by the existence of these

dual cathedrals, still more so when, as in Lombardy, the terms *Summer* and *Winter basilicas* were applied to them. Some writers think that there must have been a climatic reason for the building of a second cathedral; being smaller it would have been less drafty. However, at Milan, two baptisteries—one for men and one for women—existed before the second Cathedral of Santa Maria Maggiore was built. Both of these baptisteries were within chapels of a considerable size and had altars and choir stalls. Masses and Divine Office was celebrated in both of them. There were also several other smaller churches on the site close to the archbishopric, behind the main Cathedral of Saint Tecla. So the second cathedral was not necessary.

A fourteenth-century anonymous writer on the history of Pavia gives what I consider the clue to the solution of the problem. He mentions that all churches both large and small had screens down the middle in order to separate the men and the women. He describes the screens as being solid and without windows; there was one door in the smaller churches and three in the larger ones. The writer adds an important point: women could not see the altar except through the doorways, and these were also sometimes shut during the chanting of Divine Office.[9] The division of sexes was common until the sixteenth century. It still exists among the Copts in Abyssinia and in parts of Italy.

All big or small churches were divided by a screen with the exception of the dual cathedrals, so we are told by the Ticinese writer; the obvious reason being that the two cathedrals already served to separate the sexes, the second cathedral dedicated to Our Lady being for the women. Women always have outnumbered men in the Christian Church. Even in the Egyptian desert of the fourth century, Palladius [10] informs us that there were twenty thousand anchoresses and nuns as against the ten thousand hermits and monks. When the main cathedrals became overcrowded with women, who, furthermore, had a poor view of the liturgy, it is understandable that a second cathedral was built for them so still maintaining the division of sexes and providing enough space.

At Milan, the second Cathedral of Santa Maria Maggiore was built behind the apse of the first Cathedral of Saint Tecla and close to the women's baptistery of San Stefano al Fonte. The bap-

tistery was served by deaconnesses who lived in a house close behind. The group adopted the name Sancta Dei Genetrix Maria in
the ninth century, that is, just at the time when the Cathedral of
Santa Maria Maggiore was built.[11] It suggests that the commmu-
nity had become more closely associated with the new cathedral
dedicated to Our Lady, and as it was for women, the community
would have celebrated Divine Office there rather than exclusively
in the baptistery chapel as before.

There are many proofs of the importance of the community at
this period. In 870 (some thirty-five years after the second cathedral had been built) in a will of Bishop Garibaldi of Bergamo, the
usufruct of some houses and the full possession of others were left
to the nun Gariberga of the Monastery of Sancta Dei Genetrix
Maria called Vvigelinda, where the Abbess Alcharda presided.
The bishop left her nine slaves, a man and his wife and seven
women. They were to serve her until her death and then set
free.[12] From this document we can deduct that the community
was a big one with considerable possessions. In 903 the will of Andrea gives us further information. The Xenodochium (hospice
and hospital) founded in the house of Andrea, after passing to a
certain Varimberto, was to become subject to the close-by Monastery of Vvigelinda, together with the Church of San Rafaelo.
The Xenodochium disappeared, but the Church of San Rafaelo
remained under the jurisdiction of the nuns until the time of
Charles Borromeo.[13]

In 1005–06 another document informs us that Abbess Elena of
the Monastery of Vvigelinda gave Bishop Landolfo of Brescia
some land and a small house for the duration of twenty-nine
years from a site between the Church of San Rafaelo and their
monastery. So in the eleventh century the community still possessed land around Santa Maria Maggiore.[14]

It is recorded that in 1170, after the "Winter" cathedral had
suffered fire, the women of Milan contributed their jewels toward
the rebuilding of it. Again, in 1336, when the bell tower collapsed,
the women gave their jewels to cover the cost of reconstruction.
This shows that women considered the second cathedral their
special responsibility.[15]

It was not until the twelfth century that the community took the name of Saint Radegonda.[16] They adopted the rule of Saint Benedict; they were no longer canonesses but nuns. They were moved into a new house a small distance from the cathedral.

Archbishop Galdino of Milan, who had given them the new house, wrote a letter to the clergy of Milan [17] instructing them that it was their prerogative *alone* publicly to sing the Mass and Divine Office in the Cathedral of Santa Maria Maggiore, with the exception of the monks belonging to the congregation. They *alone* may say the Office of the Dead in the Cathedral, they *alone* may use the choir seats. No *decumani* [18] may have a seat without their special permission and invitation. The *decumani*, Galdino declares, are not priests. They may not make processions and sing psalms before any altar, with the one exception of that of Saint Ambrose. So fearful was Archbishop Galdino that the *decumani* may not obey that he issued an anathema against anyone who contravened his instructions.

Who are these *decumani* who belonged to the "Winter" basilica of Santa Maria Maggiore? These *decumani* were evidently very devout, as they were used to making processions to special altars and to taking part in the singing of the Mass and Divine Office seated in the choir stalls, and they were used to singing the Office of the Dead. None of these things could be considered reprehensible.

The *decumani* are considered by tradition to have been instituted by Saint Ambrose, and they constituted two orders of clergy in service of the diocese. The *Maiores* were drawn from the nobility and consisted of cardinals, archpriests, archdeacons, and subdeacons. They were custodians of the churches in the diocese. The *Minores* were likewise clergy, but drawn from the ordinary citizens of Milan.[19] There were seventy-two in number, plus twenty-eight from a church of Our Lady, later dedicated to San Simpliciano, called *basilica virginum;* [20] this basilica of the virgins suggests that the twenty-eight persons were women and that they were of a clerical nature. Women were listed as prebendaries in Milan in a document dated 1181.[21] They were given the title of *scriptanes*, and they are known to have been dedicated persons, although not living in community. They must, therefore, have been secular canonesses. Marcellina, the sister of Saint Ambrose, although she had taken the veil, also lived in this way. Ambrose requested her to promote the ideal of virginity among the women in Milan. They may well have been among the twenty-eight women *decumani*.

I therefore conclude that the *decumani* said by Archbishop Galvino not to be priests, and who were no longer to sing Mass or chant Divine Office from the choir stall of Santa Maria Maggiore were women.

This supposition is borne out by the old statutes of the *decumani*, which contain strange legislation and could be more easily understood if they applied to women. The document dates as late as the fifteenth century; the instructions are given under the heading: *Decumenorum vetera Statuta renovata*.[22] The *decumani* were obliged to wear a black *bireto*, a cap; the covering of the head is an injunction usual for women but not for men. The *decumani* had to say the Office of the Dead daily. Certain big feasts were excluded, among them that of Saint Elizabeth. That a woman's saint-day should be on this list is surprising; it would be more understandable for a woman's community. The special insistence on the Office of the Dead is also characteristic of women's institutes, for women have always been connected with services for the dead.

Magistretti quotes another astonishing passage in which it is said that archpresbyters of the *decumani* were not to be called prelates because they had no presidency over the Church. They were not to sit in the stalls of the prelates, nor were they to be allowed to carry a bell or a cross.[23]

All these instructions show that there was a considerable confusion as to what should or should not be done. My explanation for this confusion is that regulations intended for the canonesses of Vvigelinda were transposed from the feminine into the masculine. Giulini points out a case when the word *monachus* was wrongly used for *monachas*. Beroldus was responsible for copying the manuscripts regarding the liturgy, and little dates before his time.

The dual cathedrals in Milan came to an end when Saint Tecla was demolished to give place to a piazza in front of Santa Maria Maggiore. There was no need for dual cathedrals when not used for the segregation of the sexes. Of course, the single Cathedral of Santa Maria Maggiore was too small when it came to be used by both sexes. It was therefore enlarged and rebuilt. Today it is known as the Duomo. It was consecrated by Charles Borromeo, who also did away with the last vestiges of the regulations for *decumani*.

The significance of dual cathedrals consists in that they stand as a proof that there was a time when women's orders functioned from the choir stalls of cathedrals in the singing of the Mass and in the chanting of the Divine Office. History has been deliberately hidden so that the tradition should be lost. Women were withdrawn in the twelfth century when clergy became obliged to adopt a life of celibacy. Canonesses were required to adopt the secluded life of nuns and to celebrate their Divine Office in private chapels.

In Saint Waudru, Mons, Belgium, the clergy were not successful in turning out the canonesses. In Fontevrault the monks failed in their attempt to take over the main church and house of the nuns, and they were obliged to continue to take vows of obedience to the abbess until the time of the French Revolution. But the canonesses who once functioned together with the canons in Monza were at some time eliminated. The canonesses who were *consorores* of the canons of the Cathedral at Münster had to function from their Überwasser church, which in fact was like a double cathedral. So, by tradition women have served the Church.

In Zürich there were also two cathedrals one served by a women's order, the other by a men's order.[25] The dual cathedrals in Milan must at one time have followed the same system; that is, one of the dual cathedrals must have been served by the women's order attached to Santa Maria Maggiore—later turned out.

THE EFFECT OF THE COUNCIL OF TRENT ON THE STATUS OF WOMEN

CERTAIN DECREES of the Council of Trent were definitely detrimental to the position of women in the Church. In particular the decrees for the reform of religious orders undermined the authority of the abbesses with quasi-episcopal jurisdiction, a status they had held from time immemorial, and gave all responsibility to the bishops, leaving the abbesses in a secondary place. However, not all religious orders came under the new ordinances, so that in fact the abbesses of royal abbeys and of monasteries belonging to congregations ruled by a general chapter continued to hold their quasi-episcopal jurisdiction for yet another three hundred years, until the time of the French Revolution and even afterward.

The Council of Trent covered a period of eighteen years, from 1545 to 1564, but it was only at the last session, the twenty-fifth, held on December 3, 1563, that the decree for the reformation of religious orders for both men and women were considered. The decisions were made in haste,[1] because Pope Pius IV, who was ill, wanted to finish and close the council. He died two years later, and Pope Pius V was elected. The outcome of the Council of Trent was confused by his decision to abandon the publication of the Acts of the Council,[2] as he feared controversy between the Molinists and the Thomists.

The principle of keeping the acts secret was maintained until the nineteenth century.[3] The Marquise de Forbin d'Opède, a woman historian of the Council of Trent, who wrote under the assumed name of L. Meynièr in 1874, mentioned that there were two complete contradictory conceptions of the Council of Trent, one that adhered to the version of Paolo Sarpi, and the other to the version of Pietro Sforza Pallavicino.[4] It was not until G. Merkle, who in 1880 started to prepare the acts and decrees of the Council of Trent for publication in the Görres-Gesellschaft, that at last the full sources were revealed.[5]

It is not surprising, therefore, that there arose differences of opinion as to the ordinances of the Council of Trent, and that some bishops claimed that by the canons of the last session of the council on women's religious orders that the bishops had the right of jurisdiction over all nuns including those in exempt orders. While papal bulls such as that of Urban VIII to the Cistercian Abbey of Las Huelgas confirmed their privilege of *Nullius Diocesis*, contradicting such a claim.

The earlier bull *pericoloso* of Pope Boniface VIII was renewed in the twenty-fifth session of the council,[6] by which bishops were required to see to the strict enclosure of the nuns within their dioceses. If this ordinance was resisted, the secular arm—that is, the military—could be called in to enforce it. No nun was allowed, after profession, to go out of the convent grounds even for a brief period unless "for some lawful cause," which had to be approved by the bishop. This rule was applied also to exempt orders, that is, to orders not otherwise under the jurisdiction of the bishop.

The decree took away the quasi-episcopal abbess' responsibility over her nuns and allowed the abbey to be supervised by the bishop. Such an ordinance was a complete innovation at the time, since for many centuries certain religious orders had been granted exemption from the jurisdiction of the bishop.[7] Before the Council of Trent had made these legislations, Abbess Maria de Bretagne had brought about a very energetic reform at Fontevrault, which was continued by Abbess Renée de Bourbon.[8] Furthermore, other orders had been inspired by the reform of Fontevrault and had made similar changes. There seems, therefore, to have been no reason for giving the responsibility to bishops, since the abbesses had, with such foresight, already effected the necessary reforms. Besides, the bishops were in no better position than the abbesses to know when to grant a permission for exit; on the contrary, nuns who were the least to be trusted were able to evade the better judgment of the abbess and obtain permission to leave the grounds from the bishop who unwittingly gave it to the wrong persons. Abbess Marie Madeleine de Rouchechouart complained of this evasion of her authority to King Louis XIV. In another case the bishop withheld permission for a nun of the Abbey of Jouarre to go out to obtain proper medical attention, which brought about her death and caused great scandal.[9] Many of the bishops at the Council of Trent were against the regulations concerning the reform of women's religious orders, and some refused to sign.[10]

In Chapter 8 of the twenty-fifth session of the Council of Trent all monasteries that were not already subject to a General Chapter of a congregation and that, being directly subject to the Holy See, were not visited by the bishop of the diocese, were ordered to form themselves into a congregation within a year of the end of the council. If this were not accomplished, the metropolitan bishop was to be held responsible, as delegate of the Apostolic See, to convoke the monasteries for the purpose of forming a congregation. If necessary the monasteries could join with houses in more than one province. The congregation once formed could elect their president and arrange for the person who was to undertake the Visitation of the different houses belonging to the congregation. If any monastery did not take the measures required by the metropolitan, then it would automatically become subject to the bishop.

The custom of the Visitation of monasteries by an established person from outside the group in order to see the rule is being maintained and to see that no abuses have crept in was a system adopted from earliest times. But it had not always been considered necessary for the Visitor of women's orders to be a man— a bishop or an abbot. Mention has already been made in Chapter

6 [11] of King Edward II's request to the Abbess of Fontevrault in France to appoint his sister Mary, a nun of the Fontevrault foundation in Amesbury, Wiltshire, in England, as Visitor of the other houses of Fontevrault in England instead of sending an alien representative.[12] This was not an extraordinary request, for the king assured the abbess that his sister was capable of fulfilling such an office for she was known not to deviate from what was right when executing such Visitations; and it seems, therefore, that she had already undertaken to be Visitor on earlier occasions. In 1219 Gertrude of Lippe,[13] Abbess of Herford Abbey in Germany, undertook a long tour of monasteries with sixty-one cavalry guards to accompany her. She had the right to lodge four nights at Stockem, two nights at Schoppingen Kreishause, one at the estate owner's house, one at the priest's house, and one at Wettringen, Ibbenbüren, Lengerich, Liennen, and other places. The estate agent was expected to pay all costs of the abbess's journey, which included feeding the horses, the provision of wood to heat the rooms; and he had to guard the whole company against thieves.

To understand the jurisdiction of the quasi-episcopal abbesses it must be remembered that they were not just heads of single convents but of whole districts with often many *eigenkirche*—churches in far distant places. But with the ever increasing restrictions of enclosure, the position of the abbess changed, for she was forced to act through delegates rather than through her personal Visitations. Now, by the Council of Trent, her whole position was undermined, giving the diocesan bishop an excuse for taking over control. The ordinances of Chapter 8 of the council did not give the bishop the right of control until the monasteries had refused to form themselves into congregations, but bishops such as Bossuet made no attempt to encourage the religious orders in his diocese, either men or women, to form congregations. On the contrary, we have seen that the Abbey of Faremoutier, which attempted to join a congregation, was impeded from doing so by Bossuet, who without further ado presented himself as the apostolic delegate and enforced the abbey to accept his jurisdiction.[14] Nor did Bossuet attempt to advise the royal Abbey of Jouarre to join a congregation, but likewise forced it to accept his jurisdiction using military force as was allowed by the Council of Trent.

In 1630, Bishop Vincenzo Martinelli of Conversano,[15] and in 1659, Bishop of Palermo of Conversano both tried to obtain jurisdiction over the Cistercian Monastery of Saint Benedict's, basing their claims on the bull *inscrutabili* that was designed to put into effect the statutes of the Council of Trent. But neither bishop succeeded because the community was a member of the General Chapter of the Cistercians whose Visitors were appointed by the correct procedure of the General Chapter. The Cistercian Abbey of Las Huelgas de Burgos was likewise not affected by the injunctions of the Council of Trent.

A very short paragraph in Chapter 9 curtly lays down that nuns' orders immediately subject to the Apostolic See shall be governed by the bishops as delegates of the Apostolic See.[16] To understand the *volte-face* of this arrangement, readers are requested to return to Chapter 4 above. Orders belonging to a congregation did not come under this ruling.

The reason women's orders belonging to a congregation were made an exception to the ruling was that the abbesses even with quasi-episcopal jurisdiction already came under the ruling of the male General Superior of the whole congregation of monks and nuns, for it was generally presumed that the head of the General Chapter would be the abbot, so that the abbess would come under him. In fact, however, the Cistercian Order did not have and does not have a First and Second Order—the First Order being men and the Second Order being women—but both men's and women's orders are on an equal status. That the abbess did not *ipso facto* come under the abbot is shown by the fact that Innocent IV had to issue a bull to give an abbot the right to undertake the correction of the nuns of Las Huelgas at a certain period.[17] It would not have been necessary to issue this bull had the abbot normally the right to interfere with a woman's monastery.

The idea that women superiors should of necessity come under a higher hierarchical male superior was not approved of by all the bishops of the Council of Trent. The Bishop of Bracen [18] gave his *omnia placent* to the ordinances concerning the reform of religious orders, but with the exception that he did not like nuns being put under the care of conventual brothers as established in Chapter 9. The Bishop of Opinum in Calabria, the Bishop of Zara in Dalmatia, and the Bishop of Umbriatico in Calabria thought it wrong for a bishop to have the right to punish or correct the nuns guilty of breaking rules of enclosure.[19] Abbot Stephen of the Order of Saint Cassian wanted to remove the rule regarding nuns being put under the supervision of monks; he asked that "*omnium monialium cura monachis omnibus auferatur.*"[20] The Bishop of Verdun-sur-Meuse was against all the rules for the religious and declared: "*decretis de regularibus non placet, anathema.*"[21]

In a further decree on the right of Patronage,[22] which also affected women's orders, it was recognized as wrong to violate the pious intentions of the faithful who had made gifts of territory and goods to a religious institute by appropriating them for the use of the diocese, which indeed was what the bishops wanted to do. The orders were required to give full proofs of their rights by producing the title deeds of the property. As these communities had been in existence for many centuries during which time there had been many wars, fires, and robberies, besides other disasters, authentic documents had been lost. It was laid down that the title deeds giving the right of patronage had to be at least fifty years old. All royal patronage was to be maintained, while other estates became free and vacant.

When documents were missing, monasteries considered they had the right to forge a script by putting in what by long tradition was known to have been their right.[23] The intricate wording of these council regulations made it very easy for a person like Bossuet, an astute lawyer, to bring cases against a monastery and so produce an excuse to take the community under his jurisdiction.

Abbess Anna of Austria of Las Huelgas de Burgos was wise; she wrote personally to the Holy See to enquire in what way her abbey came under the rulings of the Council of Trent. It was then that Pope Urban VIII wrote his famous bull *Sedis apostolicae*, establishing very clearly that the Abbey of Las Huelgas was of *nullius diocesis.*

When at the time of the Council of Trent and the century afterward many women's exempt orders lost their rights and became subject to bishops, it was the royal abbeys such as Las Huelgas de Burgos, Saint Benedict of Conversano, Notre-Dame de Jouarre, and Fontevrault that were able to retain their original position. In the cases of the Abbey of Las Huelgas and Saint Benedict of Conversano, both maintained exemption not only due to their being royal abbeys but also because they each belonged to a General Chapter of the Cistercian Congregation. Most Benedictine abbeys at this time did not belong to a congregation and so were liable to come under the jurisdiction of the bishop. However, this should not have taken place unless after a reminder from the bishop the abbeys had not succeeded in forming a congregation. As at Jouarre, the bishops did not do this, and Benedictine abbeys at Brindisi, Bari, Oria, and other places in Apulia, Italy, all lost their status of independence early in the eighteenth century.[24]

Until the time of the Renaissance, when there was a return to the Greco-Roman pre-Christian culture in which women had a low status, there had been no dispute of the right of an abbess to rule over the clergy, monks and nuns, and people in her district. It had been the custom for centuries that the abbess, who was generally a member of a royal family, to rule over her territory in the same way as a queen or a king, an empress or emperor. The Byzantine empresses and emperors had spiritual as well as temporal jurisdiction in their countries, so it was nothing new for an abbess likewise to have spiritual and temporal jurisdiction in the territories over which she ruled as a sovereign in church and civil matters.

The theological concept was not developed early by which it was thought necessary for a woman, even when superior, to be ultimately dependent on a male in a higher hierarchical position. Later, the right of the abbess to have dominion over churches in her territory was considered dependent on her having been delegated to the office by the Holy See, that is, by the pope, a male superior. Mongelli considered that such a delegation was an abuse. According to this view some two hundred popes who accepted the right of abbesses to exercise quasi-episcopal jurisdiction had been guilty of permitting an abuse, as against only eight popes who since the time of Pius IX have denied abbesses this right.

Although many abbesses have held quasi-episcopal jurisdiction during many centuries, it was not until 1638 that a theologian, Tamburini,[25] produced a complete treatise on the nature of the authority of the abbesses, which with a lawyer's dexterity he sought to explain away.

CONCLUSION

The decrees of the Council of Trent regarding the reform of religious orders was rushed through without proper time for discussion and without unanimity of opinion, for some bishops were strongly against the reforms, especially those stipulating that women's orders be supervised by men's orders. The strict enclosure had very damaging effects on the general culture of the women's orders, and the authority of the abbess was bypassed. The age-long custom of the exemption of certain orders from jurisdiction of the bishop of the locality was undermined by making the bishops themselves the apostolic delegates. It was a legal evasion of the ruling that had been sustained by literally hundreds of pontiffs.

The right of abbesses to rule was not questioned until the time of the Renaissance, when there was a return to a Greco-Roman culture in which women had had a lower status than in Christian times. Robert Abrissel's ideal in his foundation of Fontevrault by which the priests and monks of the order took vows of obedience to the abbess in imitation of the obedience of Christ to his mother, as well as of Saint John, the Virgin's adopted son, was lost and forgotten.

The post-Trentine theologians sought to establish the inability of abbesses to hold spiritual jurisdiction on the basis of their inability to be ordained to the order of the priesthood; but they violated historical facts by denying that women were ordained as clerical members in the Canoness Institutes to say the Divine Office, the part of the Church Service that did not entail touching the blessed Eucharist. The ordination of an archdeaconess and of a *Sacerdos Maxima* did allow women to have spiritual jurisdiction. In the case of Las Huelgas this right was manitained until 1874.

FINAL CONCLUSION

It has been established that there has been an authentic tradition of women's service to the Church that has become hidden. The

Church has shown itself versatile in adapting itself to various forms of government—oligarchic, monarchic, and democratic. There is no reason why women should not hold a type of responsibility today similar to that of the quasi-episcopal status of abbesses in the past. The desirability of small dioceses has been generally approved. The inclusion of women within the episcopal hierarchy again would make the multiplication of dioceses easier.

The fact that women were not ordained to the consecration of the Eucharist is a tradition of long standing, but based on a quite erroneous scientific understanding of genetics. It would be ridiculous to continue a tradition based on such a fallacy. To maintain that only men can represent Christ in the act of sacrifice is carrying an analogy too far. If only men can represent Christ, then only women can represent the Church—the spouse of Christ. But in baptism there is no discrimination of the sexes. Women as well as men are "other Christs," men as well as women can by unity in the Holy Spirit represent the spouse of Christ.

How do we hope that such a change of attitude may be brought about? Not by marching about with banners demanding our right. The Book of Genesis explains the domination of man over woman as the result of the Fall and of sin. There is therefore a need for man to act against this tendency and to take steps to correct it. As Jesus Christ crowns Mary, so man should crown womankind.

The crowning of Mary is a symbolic way of expressing a recognition of her cooperation in salvation through her constant unity with the Holy Spirit. By baptism, both men and women tend again to a primeval perfection, and together in the Holy Spirit they should promote salvation in the world, and cooperate in the service of God and in worship.

NOTES

DALC. *Dictionnaire d'archéologie chrétienne et de liturgie*, F. Cabrol (ed.) (Paris, 1912–1955).

PG. *Patrologia Graeca*, J. P. Migne (ed.), 161 vols. (Paris, 1857–1866).

PL. *Patrologia Latina*, J. P. Migne (ed.), 221 vols. (Paris, 1879–1890).

CHAPTER ONE

1. I Corinthians 10:11.
2. Acts 16:14–15, 40.
3. Acts 12:12.
4. Colossians 4:15.
5. Romans 16:3, 5; I Corinthians 16:19; I Corinthians 16:15, 17, the name of Stephana put before the name of Fortunatus.
6. Clement of Alexandria, *Paedagogi*, P.G. 8, lib. 3, col. 675 D.ff. "*Plurima autem alia praecepta, quae ad ELECTA PERSONAS pertinent, in sanctis libris scripta sunt: haec quidam presbyteris, alia vero episcopis, alia diaconis, alia autem VIDUIS, de quibus fuerit aliud dicendi tempus.*"
7. See Appendix I.
8. Pliny the Younger, *Epistles 96 and 97*.
9. Mary Bateson, *Origin and Early History of Double Monasteries*, transactions of the Royal History Society (London: Longman, Green and Co., 1899), vol. 13.
10. See Chapter Three.
11. *The Jerusalem Bible* (London: Darton, Longman and Todd, 1966) translates *episcopus* as "overseers" in Acts 20:28.

CHAPTER TWO

1. J. B. de Rossi, *Musaici Cristiani delle Chiese di Roma* (Rome: Libreria Spithöver di G. Haass, 1899), vol 7, p. 4 of the notes for plate XXVI of the mosaics of the "Oratorio di S. Zenone."

2. O. Marucchi, *Élement d'Archéologie chretienne, III, Basiliques et Églises de Rome* (Paris: Desclée, 1902), p. 325.

3. Antonio Bosio, *Roma Sotteraneo* (Rome: Carlo Aldobrandiso, 1632), chap. XX, p. 123 D.ff.

4. II Timothy 4:21.

5. F. Grossi-Gondi, *Trattato di Epigrafia Cristiana* (Rome: Università Gregoriana, 1920), p. 153.

6. G. Marini, *Inscriptiones Christianes*, Ms. Vat. 9072, part II, chap. XXII, no. i, 1608 (1904).

7. *Ibid.*, chap. XXII.

8. *Ibid.*, chap. XXII, p. 427.

9. *Ibid.*, p. 423.

10. Le Nain de Tillemont, *Mémoires pour servir à l'Histoire Ecclésiastique* (Paris: 1720).

11. St. John Chrysostom, *homily* 67.

12. Justinian, *Novellae*, chap. XXX, "Diaconissam," ed. G. Kroll (Berlin: Weidermannde Verlag, 1954), vol. 3.

13. See Appendix I.

14. Benedict Aniani, *Concordia Regularum*, PL. 103, col. 950.

15. See Appendix V.

CHAPTER THREE

1. Acts 9:36.

2. Mary Lawrence McKenna, *Women of the Church Role and Renewal* (New York: P. J. Kenedy & Sons, 1967), p. 43.

3. Vincent McNabb, "Was the Rule of St. Augustine Written for Melania the Younger," *Journal of Theological Studies* (London: 1919) vol. 20, pp. 242–49.

4. See p. 63.

5. See pp. 132 ff.

6. L. Deviller, *Chartes du Chapitre de Sainte Waudru de Mons* (Brussels: Archives de Hainaut; Mons: Archives de l'État, 1884–1906), 2 vols.

7. See p. 64 ff.

8. Deviller, *op. cit.*, p. 54; Jacques de Guise, *Annals de Hainaut*, Ms. Reg. 9243 Bibliothèque Royale de Bruxelles, fol. 288.

9. Ernest Matthieu, *Mons à Travers-les-Ages* (Mons: Léon Dequesne, 1921), p. 53; information taken from Giselbert, *Chronica*, ed. Godefroy Menelglaise, T. L.

10. Antonio Francesco Frisi, *Memorie delle Chiese Monzese* (Milan: Galeazzi Regio stampatore, 1774), Dissitazione quarta, p. 92.

11. See Appendix VII.

12. C. Butler, *The Lausiac History of Palladius* (Cambridge: Texts and Studies, 1898), p. 212.

13. M. L. McClure and C. L. Feltoe, *The Pilgrimage of Etheria* (London: Palestine Pilgrim Text Society, 1897), p. 42 ff.
14. E. Herzfeld, "Marianilik," *Monumenta Asia Antiquis*, American Society for Archeological Research (Oxford: University Press, 1930), vol 2, pp. 1–88; J. Keil and A. Wilhelm, "Denkmäler aus dem Rauhen Kilkien" (1931), vol. 3.
15. See Appendix V.
16. Mary Bateson, *Origin and Early History of Double Monasteries*, transaction of the Royal History Society (London: Longman, Green and Co., 1899), vol. 13.
17. Luke 8:1–2.
18. See Appendix II.
19. Saint Gregory of Nyssa, *Vita Santa Macrina*, PG. 46, col. 960 ff; W. K. Lowther Clarke, *The Life of St. Macrina by Gregory of Nyssa* (London, S.P.C.K., 1916).
20. St. Gregory of Nazianzus, *Epistle 197*, English translation in Ante-Nicene Fathers. S. II., vol. 7.
21. Cogitosus, "Vita Sanctae Brigidae" in Thomas Messingham, *Florilegium Insulae Sanctorum seu Vitae et Acta Sanctorum Hiberniae* (Paris: Cramoise, 1624), chap. VI, p. 193 ff.
22. See Appendix I.
23. *Documents Officiels inédits sur l'histoire des Églises de Sainte Waudru et de St. Germain à Mons* (Mons: Archives communale de l'État, Société des Bibliophiles belges, 1843), no. 23, p. 88 ff.

CHAPTER FOUR

1. Procopius of Ceasarea, *The Secret History of the Court of the Emperor Justinian* (London: English translation printed by John Barkesdale, 1674), chaps. X and XVI.
2. See Appendix IV.
3. See Appendix VIII.
4. Dorothy Whitelock, *English Documents* (London: Eyre and Spottiswoode, 1955), vol. I, p. 651.
5. Jean Mabillon, *Annalis S. Benedicti* (Paris: Lutechlae, 1703–1739), p. 687. These bulls are often suspected of being fabricated at a later period than claimed; even so the formula shows what was considered to be the custom.
6. D. P. Mansi, *Sacrorum Conciliorum*, Nova Editio, vols. 12 and 13 on seventh General Council.
7. See p. 19.
8. Bede, *op. cit.*, Book III; Cogitosus, "Vita Sanctae Brigidae" in Thomas Messingham, *Florilegium Insulae Sanctorum seu Vitae et Acta Sanctorum Hiberniae* (Paris: Cramoise, 1624), chap. VI,

p. 193 ff; J. Ryan, *Irish Monasticism* (London: Longman, Green and Co., 1931), pp. 163–90.

9. Caesarius, "Regula Virginum," *Codex Regularum Monasticarum,* ed. Holsten and Brockie (Augsburg: 1759), vol. 2.

10. St. Gregory the Great, *Epistola XII;* PL. 77–78. The Vatican Ms. D. adds: *"Sivi de suis elegerit ordinatur"* left out of other Mss. which shows a prejudice against women being ordained, even though here the ordination did not entail priesthood.

11. See p. 65. The Abbess of the Canoness Institute of St. Mary's Überwasser was archdeaconess and was able to represent the bishop in several towns.

12. See Appendix V. George Fabricius gave the title of *Sacerdos Maxima* and *Sacerdotes Virgines* to some twenty abbesses and canonesses or nuns in his *Saxon Chronicles.*

13. See p. 18.

14. The term women's "monastery" is used in this book in preference to "nunnery" or "convent" because in the Middle Ages many women's monasteries covered large districts over which the abbesses ruled as well as over their own communities. They were very different to convent communities today.

15. See Chapter Nine on the Abbey of Las Huelgas, Burgos.

16. D. Knowles, "The Growth of Exemption" in "Essays in Monastic History," *Downside Abbey Review* (1932), vol. 1, pp. 201–31; Giles Constable, chap. on "Growth of Monastic Freedom" in *Monastic Tithes* (Cambridge: Studies in Medieval Life and Thought, 1964), vol. 10; Terence P. McLaughlin, *Le Très Ancien Droit Monastique de l'Occident* (Ligugé: Abbaye St. Martin. Paris: A. Pacard, 1935); Jean-François Lemarignier, *L'Étude sur les Privilèges d'Exemption et Jurisdiction Ecclesiastique des Abbayes Normandes* (Paris: A. Pacard, Archives de la France Monastique, 1937); D. Z. B. Van Espen, *Jus Ecclesiasticum Universum* (Louvain: 1784), Tom. 1, Tit. 33, chap. 2, no. 31.

17. Vatican Ms. Reg. 17 and 18; Lucien Auvray, *Les Registres de Gregoire IX* (Paris: Bibliothèque des Écoles Françaises d'Athène et de Rome, 1896–1910), vols. 1 and 2 and Fascicule XII (1910).

18. Lucien Auvray. *Ibid.,* vol. 1, p. 254. January 26, 1230.

19. *Ibid.,* vol. 1, p. 55. June 12, 1227.

20. *Ibid.,* vol. 1, p. 279. April 27, 1230.

21. *Ibid.,* Fascicule XII, p. 290. July 19, 1240.

22. *Ibid.,* Fascicule XII, p. 298. August 11, 1240.

23. *Ibid.,* Fascicule XII, p. 346. January 23, 1241.

24. *Ibid.,* Fascicule XII, p. 493. April 26, 1241.

25. *Ibid.,* vol. 1, no. 1194, p. 676. March 8, 1233.

26. See Chapter Eight on the Cistercian Abbey of St. Benedict, Conversano.

27. Vatican Ms. Reg. 17. Epistle 44, A.D. 1235.

1. Venerable Bede, *A History of the English Church and People*, trans. Leo Sherley-Price (Victoria, Australia: Penguin Books, 1956), book IV, chaps. XXI, XXIII.

2. Charles Reid Peers and Courteny Arthur Ralegh, "The Saxon Monastery of Whitby," *Archeologia* (London: Society of Antiquaries, series 2, 1943), vol. 89.

3. A. W. Haddon and W. P. Stubbs, *Councils and Ecclesiastical Documents Relating to Great Britain and Ireland* (Oxford: Clarendon Press, 1871), vol. 3, p. 264; Dorothy Whitelock, *English Documents* (London: Eyre and Spottiswoode, 1955), vol. 1, p. 695.

4. Bede, *op. cit.*, book IV, chap. 25.

5. See Chapter Six.

6. *Ibid.*

7. *Liber Eliensis*, ed. D. J. Stewart (London: Impensis Societatis, 1848), chap. XXV, p. 761.

8. *Ibid.*, p. 78.

9. Jean Mabillon, *Acta Sanctorum Saeculum* (Paris: 1703), vol. 2, p. 758.

10. See p. 18.

11. Gregory the Great, *Epistola XII*; PL. 77–78; see p. 18.

12. Haddon and Stubbs, *op. cit.*, vol. 3, p. 240.

13. Egerton Ms. 2104a, British Museum.

14. W. Dugdale, *Monasticarum Anglicanum* (London: John Bohn, 1846), vol. 2, pp. 634–37.

15. *Ibid.*, p. 638.

16. See below p. 47.

17. Frederick Ernest Kettner, *Antiquitates Quedlinburgenses* (Leipzig: Verlegts J. Christ, Konig, 1712), p. 231. Bull sent to the Archbishop of Saxony from Honorius III, A.D. 1220.

18. Victoria History of Counties, "Doomsday Survey," Hampshire, vol. 1, p. 399 ff.

19. Tanner, *Notitia Monastica*, Dorset XXIII, note r quoted by Dugdale, *op. cit.*, vol. 2, p. 472.

20. *Victoria History of Counties*, Derby II (London: Archibald Constable, 1907), p. 43.

21. W. Holtzmann, *Papsturkunden in England* (Berlin: Abhandlungen der Gesellschaft der Wissenschaften zu Göttingen, 1952), dritte folge 33, nos. 362, 363.

22. H. F. Chettle, *English Houses of the Order of Fontevrault*, reprinted from *Downside Review*, vol. 70 (1942).

23. Holtzmann, *op. cit.*, no. 283.

24. *Ibid.*, no. 95, Chartular, S. XIII, fol 2.

25. *Ibid.*, no. 236.

26. W. O. Hassal, ed., *Cartulary of St. Mary Clerkenwell* (London:

Royal History Society, Camden, 3rd series, 1949), vol. 71, p. vii.

27. R. R. Sharpe, *Court of Husting Calendar of Wills Husting Roll* (London: Archives of the Corporation of London, 1890), vol. 2, pp. 304–306. January 25, 1393–1394.

28. *The Register of Henry Chichele, Archbishop of Canterbury*, edited by E. F. Jacob (Oxford: Clarendon Press, 1947), vol. 1, pp. 194, 220.

29. See Chapter Seven.

30. *Calendar of Patent Rolls. Edward VI*, vol. 3, 1549–1551 (London: His Majesties Stationary Office, 1925), pp. 171–72.

31. W. Holtzmann, *op. cit.*, Phil. Hist. Klasse. 1925, Neue Folg 25.

32. See Appendix V.

33. David Knowles and R. N. Hadcock, *Medieval Religious Houses in England and Wales* (London: Longman Group, 1971—latest edition; first edition 1953).

CHAPTER SIX

1. *L'Abbaye Royale Notre-Dame de Jouarre*, by 12 authors, preface by M. Aubert (Paris: Bibliothèque d'Histoire et d'Archéologie Chrétiennes, 1961); M. Troussaint Duplessis, *Histoire de l'Église de Meaux* (Paris: Gaudouin and Giffart, 1731), 2 vols.; Mabillon, *Annales*, Tom. I (1703), p. 364 ff. *Acts SS Benedict*, p. 221; Desguerrois, *La Saincteté chrétienne* (Troyes: 1637); Jean Hubert, *Les Cryptes de Jouarre* (Melun: IV Congrès de l'art du Haut Moyen Age, 1952); *L'Art Préroman* (Paris: Les Éditions d'Art et Histoire, 1938); Maurice Lecompte, *Abbaye et prieurés de l'ancien diocèse de Meaux* (Meaux: 1899); H. Thiercelin, *Les Monastères de Jouarre* (Paris: Congrés Archéologique de France, 1861); E. Jovy, *Le Correspondence de Bossuet*, (Paris: Urbain et Levesque, 1921), vol. 3.

2. Jonas, PL. 87, col. 1011.

3. *Abbaye de N.D. de Jouarre*, vol. 1, pp. 13–18; Desguerrois, *op. cit.*

4. Jean Hubert, *op. cit.*

5. Register of Clementis V, nos. 5245–5240 mentioned by Duplessis, *op. cit.*, Tom. II.

6. *Abbaye de N.D. de Jouarre*, vol. 1, p. 75.

7. *Ibid.*, p. 79.

8. See p. 2.

9. Duplessis, *op. cit.*, Tom. I, p. 141.

10. See p. 25.

11. Jean-François Lemarignier, *L'Étude sur les Privilèges d'Exemption et Jurisdiction Ecclésiastiques des Abbayes Normandes* (Paris: A. Pacard. Archives de la France Monastique, 1937), p. 136.

12. Duplessis, *op. cit.*, vol. 2, p. 24.
13. Bull of John IV in Jaffé, *Regesta Pontificarum Romanorum*, no. 2084.
14. Bull of Martin I, cited by Duplessis, *op. cit.*, p. 677.
15. *Abbaye de N.D. de Jouarre*, vol. 1, p. 95; Duplessis, *op. cit.*, vol. 1, p. 205.
16. *Abbey de N.D. de Jouarre*, vol. 1, p. 95.
17. A. Potthast, *Regestra Pontificarum Romanorum* (Berolini: 1874), nos. 1351, 1352.
18. *Abbaye de N.D. de Jouarre*, vol. 1, p. 95.
19. Potthast, *op. cit.*, nos. 2069, 2433.
20. Register of Pope Honorius III, Reg. Vat. 13, fol. 44–44v; Potthast, *op. cit.*, no. 1782.
21. *Abbaye Royale de N.D. de Jouarre*, vol. 1, p. 97.
22. *Abbaye de N.D. de Jouarre*, vol. 1, p. 258 from the Ms. in the Bibliothèque Nationale, fr. 15697, pp. 226–31.
23. *Abbaye de N.D. de Jouarre*, vol. 1, 260; see also Appendix VIII.
24. See Appendix VIII.
25. *Abbaye de N.D. de Jouarre*, vol. 1, p. 280.
26. Simone Poignant, *L'Abbaye de Fontevrault et les Filles de Louis XV* (Paris: Nouvelles Éditions Latines, 1966).
27. G. A. Lobineau, *Histoire de la Bretagne* (Paris: chez la veuve Françoise Muguet, 1707), vol. 1, p. 151.
28. H. Nicquet, S. J., *Histoire de L'Ordre de Fontevrault* (Paris: Michel Soley, 1642), pp. 218 ff; Poignant, *op. cit.*, p. 20.
29. Nicquet, *op. cit.*, p. 218.
30. *Calendar of Close Rolls*, Edward II (1317), p. 470.
31. Serrano, *Cartulario de Monasterio de Vega*, (Madrid: Centros de Estudios Históricos, 1927).
32. Poignant, *op. cit.*, p. 24.
33. Bibl. d'Angers, Ms. 880 (792) quoted by Poignant, *op. cit.*, p. 25.
34. Nicquet, *op. cit.*, pp. 279–780.
35. Bibl. Nat. Paris, Ms. Lat. 5480–1, f. 391; 5480–2, ff. 271–73, quoted by Poignant, *op. cit.*, p. 30.
36. *Ibid.*, p. 38.
37. Rabelais, *Pantagruel*, (Chicago: Encyclopaedia Britannica, 1952). Book III, chap. 34.
38. Bibl. Nat. Paris, Ms. Fr. 14435: *Règle de Marie de Bretagne*.
39. Poignant, *op. cit.*, p. 45.
40. Nicquet, *op. cit.*, pp. 348–49.
41. Bibl. Nat. Paris, Lat. 5480–2, f. 33, quoted by Poignant, *op. cit.*, p. 55.
42. *Ibid.*, p. 82.
43. *Ibid.*, p. 83.
44. Bibl. Nat. Imprimés LD 16.183; Poignant, *op. cit.*, p. 84.

45. See p. 101.
46. See p. 85 and Appendix VI.
47. Poignant, *op. cit.*, p. 85 ff.
48. *Ibid.*, p. 89.
49. *Ibid.*, p. 91.
50. *Ibid.*, p. 92.
51. Bibl. Nat. Paris, impr. LD 17.117 quoted by Poignant, *op. cit.*, p. 97.
52. Arch. Municipal de Fontevrault, *Registre de la paroisse* cadestre. fol. 30 v.
53. *Ibid.*, *Registre des Citoyens actives Délibérations*, fol. 30 v.
54. See p. 59.
55. *Revue Mabillon* (Abbaye de Ligugé, Chevelogne, Belgium: Archives de la France), nos. IX and X "Documents de l'Abbaye de Sainte Croix." May 1911, August 1911, November 1911, February 1912.
56. *Analecta Juris Pontifici*, t.X, p. 404, April 25, 1072. Quoted from *Revue Mabillon*, vol. 9, p. 52.
57. Wiederhold, *Papstkunder in Frankreich*, Fasc. VI, p. 35. Quoted from *Revue Mabillon*, vol. 9.
58. P. de Monsabert, *Le Monastère de Saint-Croix* (Poitiers: 1952), pp. 9–10.

CHAPTER SEVEN

1. See Appendix V, p. 130 ff.
2. F. E. Kettner, *Kirchen und Reformations Hist. des Kaiserl. Freien Weltlichen Stifts Quedlinburg* (Quedlinburg: Theodorus Jeremias Schwan, 1710), p. 32.
3. See p. 12.
4. See p. 10.
5. Kettner, *op. cit.*, p. 2. "*inferiores Familiarum collegiones.*"
6. Kettner, *Antiquitates Quedlinburgenses* (Leipzig: 1712), pp. 39–42. See also above pp. 12 and 54–57.
7. *Ibid.*, p. 42.
8. *Ibid.*, p. 200.
9. Edmund E. Stengel. "Die Grabschrift der ersten Abtissin von Quedlinburg" (Weimar: *Deutches Archives für Geschichte des Mittelalter*, Verlag H. Böhlaus, 3 1. Abt. 1939), p. 164 ff.
10. Kettner, *op. cit.*, p. 116.
11. J. Fritsch, *Geschichte des vormaligen Reichstifts und den Stadt Quedlinburg* (Quedlinburg: Verlag von G. Wasse, 1828), vol. 1, p. 5.
12. Charters Ant. Parl. 73 Lord Keeper Williams. Ms. 25 in the British Museum.
13. See Appendix V.

14. Kettner, *Antiquitates Quedlinburgenses*, p. 227 ". . . *quam idem Episcopus utpote nullum habens in eas jurisdictionem ordinariam vel etiam delegatem, . . .*"

15. *Ibid.*, p. 230. ". . . *in praeceptis dare nostris literis dignaremur, ne contra Privilegia Pontificum Romanorum tam idem monasterium, quam ipsius membra super bonis eorum seu rebus Clericorum ac Laicorum ac dictum Monasterium pertinentibus praesumant de cetero molestare.*"

16. *Ibid.*, p. 222.

17. *Ibid.*, p. 19.

18. Fritsch, *op. cit.*, vol 2.

19. Kettner, p. 660.

20. See Appendix V, p. 130.

21. *Summa Theologica*, II. II. Q. 189, a. 8. ad. 2; Q. 189. a. 8. ad. 2; Q. 184. ad. 8; Q. 194. a. 8.

22. Suarez, quoted by A. Allaria in an article on "Canons and Canoness Regulars" *Catholic Encyclopedia* (New York: R. Appleton & Co., 1908), vol 3, p. 296.

23. See Appendix VII.

24. *Ms. Evangelia Überwasser*, Münster Staat Archives, VII, 1007a; Franz von Darp, *Die Herberegister des Klosters Überwasser und des Stifts St. Mauritz*, Codex Traaditionem Westf (Münster: 1888) Bd. III; Rudolf Schulze, *Das adelige Frauen-(Kanonissen-) Stift der Hl. Maria und Die Pfarre Liebfrauen-Überwasser zu Münster Westfalen* (Münster: Verlag der Westfalischen Voreindruckerei, 1926) p. 23. (Later publication: Verlag Ashendorff; Münster: Westfalen, 1952).

25. Deviller, Chartres du Chapitre de Sainte Waudru de Mons (Brussels: Archives de Hainaut; Mons: Archives de L'Etat, 1884–1906), p. 43.

26. K. H. Schäfer, *Die Kanonissenstifter im Deutschen Mittelalter* (Amsterdam: Verlag P. Schippers N. V., 1965), p. 208.

27. *Ms. Evangelia Überwasser.*

28. Schulze, *op. cit.*, p. 31.

29. *Ibid.*, p. 27.

30. *Ibid.*, p. 44.

31. *Ibid.*, p. 145 ff.

32. *Ibid.*, p. 225.

CHAPTER EIGHT

1. Auvray, *op. cit.*, p. 1194.

2. Domenico Morea and Francisco Muciaccia, *Le Pergamene di Conversano* (Trani: R. Deputazione di Storia Patria per le Puglie, Codice Diplomatico Barese, 1943), vol. 27, Nuovo Seria.

3. *Ibid.*, Introduction, p. x.

4. Giovanni Mongelli, *Le Abbadesse Mitrate di S. Benedetto di Conversano* (Edizione del Santuario Montevergine, 1960).
5. Morea e Muciaccia, *op. cit.*, perg. 5, p. 7.
6. *Ibid.*, perg. 6 and 7, pp. 8–10.
7. *Ibid.*, perg. 16, pp. 21–22; F. Ughelli, *Italia Sacra* (Venice: apud S. Coleti, 1721), vol. 7, pp. 707–708.
8. See pp. 84–85.
9. Morea e Muciaccia, *op. cit.*, perg. 21–23, pp. 31–35.
10. Mongelli, *op. cit.*, p. 57.
11. *Ibid.*, pp. 90–91.
12. *Ibid.*, p. 93.
13. *Ibid.*, p. 97 ff.
14. *Ibid.*, p. 98.
15. *Ibid.*, p. 102.
16. S. Simone, *Il Mostro della Puglia* ossia *La Storia del celebre Monastero di S. Benedetto di Conversano* (Bari: 1885). The full text of the letter is published in the Appendix.
17. *Guide of Brindisi* (Brindisi: 1890).
18. *Codice Diplomatici di Brindisi* (Brindisi: Biblioteca Annibale de Leo). Three volumes containing documents between A.D. 492–1499; D. Annibale de Leo, *Dell' Antichissima Città di Brindisi e Oria* (Napoli, 1846); *Codice Diplomatici Barese* (Bari: Biblioteca Nationale), vols. 1–17; Mario Falco, "La Soppressione dei Conventi," *Rivista d'Italia*, Anno XIII, vol. 1, no. 5, 1914.
19. Ms. Vat. Reg. 17. *Epistles*; L. Auvray, vol. 1, no. 1194, p. 676, March 8, 1233; see p. 22.
20. Pier Fausto Palumbo, "Il Monastero Normano di S. Giovanni Evangelista," *Archivio Storico Pugliese*, 5, 1952, 43, p. 133.
21. See p. 62 and pp. 137–138.
22. K. H. Schäfer, *Die Kanonissenstifter im Deutschen Mittelalter* (Amsterdam: Verlag P. Schippers N. V., 1965), chap. 17, p. 169.

CHAPTER NINE

1. Amancio Rodríguez López, *El Real Monasterio de Las Huelgas de Burgos y el Hospital del Rey* (Burgos: Centro Catolico, 1907); Ángel Manrique, *Cisterciensium seu verius ecclesiasticorum annalium a condito Cistercio* (Lugduni: 1642) Tom. III.; José Maria Escrivá, *La Abadesa de las Huelgas* (Madrid: Editorial Luz, 1944).
2. Bull of Clement III, 1187 confirmed the foundation, a second bull, 1188, gave exemption. (Archives of the Abbey de Las Huelgas, no. 30 in no. 5.)
3. M. A. E. Wood, *Lives of the Princesses of England from the Norman Conquest* (London: Henry Colburn, 1849), vol. 1.
4. Manrique, *Cist. Annalium* (1589), vol. 3, chap. IV.

5. Archives of the Abbey, Leg. 7, 261, ARM.

6. Francesco de Berganza, *Antigüedades de España* (Francesco del Hierro, 1721) Part II, Libro VI, Cap. 6.

7. Manrique, *Cist. Annalium*, vol. 3, p. 245.

8. Rodríguez, *op. cit.*, vol. 1, pp. 107–108.

9. Venerable Bede, in a commentary on Ezra, quoted by Plummer, vol. 2, p. 245.

10. Juliano Paris, *Monasticon Cisterciense* (Solesmis: 1892), p. 389.

11. M. Colmeiro, *Historia General de España*, vol. 12, p. 162 ff.

12. Conde de Castilia Garci-Fernandes, *Fundación de la Abadía del Infantado de Covarrubias*, original Ms. in the archives of Covarrubias, Leg I. no. 10, published in L. Serrano, *Fuentes para la Historia de Castilla* (Valladolid: Casa Editorial Cuesta, 1907), vol. 2, p. 36.

13. Schäfer, *op. cit.*, p. 252.

14. Archives of the Abbey of Las Huelgas, no. 75.

15. Menéndez Pidal, ed., *Primera Crónica General de Las Huelgas*, (Madrid: 1898), p. 720.

16. Higini Anglès, *El Codes Musical de Las Huelgas* (Barcelona: Institude d'Estudes Catalans, Biblioteca de Catalana, 1931), 3 vols.

17. Lucian Serrano, *Una Estigmatizada Cisterciense Doña Antonia Jacinta de Navarra y de la Cueva* (Burgos: Librería del Centro Católico, 1924).

18. N. D. Shergold, *A History of the Spanish Stage* (Oxford: Clarendon Press, 1967), p. 446 mentions girls of twelve performing in plays as being quite a common thing.

19. Archives of the Abbey, Leg. 54, no. 7.

20. Archives of the Abbey, Leg. 7, no. 261 (1629).

21. Rodríguez, *op. cit.*, vol. 2, p. 206 ff.

22. *Ibid.*, Appendix no. 32, p. 332.

23. Pius IX, *Pontificis Maximi Acta* (Vatican: 1873), vol. 6.

CHAPTER TEN

1. Jasper Ridley, *John Knox* (Oxford: Clarendon Press, 1968) p. 179.

2. See Appendix VIII.

3. See Appendix VIII.

4. A. Tamburini, *"de iure Abbatissarum et Monialium"* (Rome: 1638).

5. *Ibid.*, p. 359 ff.

6. A. Z. B. Van Espen, *Jus Ecclesiasticum Universum* (Louvain: 1753), Tit. XXXIII, chap. II, p. 355 ff.

7. Bertrandus Loth, *Resolutionibus Belgias*, Tract 9, Q. 2, Art. 2, quoted by Van Espen, *op. cit.*

8. É. Lairtuliers, *Les Femmes de la Révolution* (Paris: 1900).

9. Leopold Lacour, "Rose Lacombe," *Revue Hebdomodaire* (Paris: 1899).

10. Maxime, *L'Ésprit de La Législation Napoléonienne* (Paris: 1898).

1. M. M. Knight and I. Lowther Peters, *Taboo and Genetics* (London: Kegan Paul & Co., 1921), Part II.
2. *Zend-Avesta*, Sacred Books of the East Series, (Oxford: 1880–1883).
3. Pliny the Elder, *Natural History*, Book XXVIII, chap. XXIII, 78–80; Book VII, Chapter 65 (Trans. by W. H. S. Jones, Loeb Classical Library, 1963).
4. Shakuntala Rao Shastri, *Women in the Vedic Age* (Bombay: Bharatiya Vidya Bhaven, 1960), p. 80.
5. Rabbi Dr. I. Epstein, *The Babylonian Talmud, Sedar Toboreth*, Toboreth II, chap. VII, Mishnah 1 (London: Socino Press, 1948), p. 399.
6. *Ibid.*, p. 401.
7. *Ibid.*, p. 366.
8. *Ibid.*, p. 122.
9. Herbert Danby, *Code of Maimonides* (Yale: Judaic Series, 1954), vol. 8.
10. F. X. Funk, ed. *Diddscalia et Constitutiones Apostolorum* (Paderbornae: Lib. F. Schoening, 1905), vols. 1, 6, 22, 2–5, pp. 376–78.
11. Gregory the Great, *Epistle LXIV*, P.L. 77, col. 1183, Tenth Interrogation, col. 1193.
12. Matthew 9:18ff.
13. Gregory the Great, *op. cit.*
14. Haddon and Stubbs, "Theodore's Penitential" IX, p. 189, in *Councils and Eccl. Documents.*
15. Bede, *History of the English Church*, Book I.
16. Haddon and Stubbs, *op. cit.*, p. 32.
17. Duplessis, *Histoire de l'Église de Meaux*, Synod de Meaux, 1493.
18. PL. XXV, col. 1517.
19. *Epistle XLVIII*, PL. XXII, col. 505.
20. *Quaeast. in Haptateuchum* III, chap. 64, PL. XXXIV, col. 706; also PL. XLIV, col. 199.
21. Peter Browne, S.J., *Beiträge zur Sexualithik des Mittel-Alters* (Breslau: Studien zur historischen Theologie, F.X. Seppelt. 23.1932).
22. Mansi, *Sacrorum Conciliorum*, editio Novissime (Venice: 1774), vol. 19, p. 181: "*Liber Legum Ecclesiasticarum*" ex Ms. Colleg. Chr. Cantabr. S XVIII, VI. "*Ut Femina ad altare in celebratione non accedant*" "*Injungimus etiam, ut iis temporibus, quibus presbyter missam celebrat, nulla mulier approprinquet altari, sed in suo loco, et presbyter ibi ab illa oblationem accipiat, quam Deo offerre velit. Mulieres recordari debent infirmitatis suae et sexus sui im-*

becillitatis, et ideo cavare debent, ne alquid illarum sacrarum rerum immundent, quae ad ecclesiae ministerium pertinent."

Appendix II

1. Mark 4:31–44; Luke 9:10–17; John 6:1–13.
2. Matthew 14:21.
3. Luke 8:1–3.
4. Mark 15:40–41.
5. Luke 8:3
6. Matthew 4:22.
7. See p. 113, references in note 4.
8. Rossi, *op. cit.*, vol. 7.
9. John 4:1–42.
10. John 11:5.
11. John 8:1–11.
12. E. O. James, *Marriage Customs Through the Ages* (New York: The Macmillan Co., 1965), p. 109.
13. Matthew 22:1–13.
14. Luke 11:42–52.
15. Cecil Roth, *The Haggadah* (London: Soncino Press), Introduction, p. vii.
16. Luke 22:17–20.

Appendix III

1. Acts 8:3.
2. Acts 17:11–15.
3. Acts 16:14–15.
4. Acts 16:40.
5. See Chapter One.
6. Acts 17:11.
7. Acts 17:12.
8. Romans 16:1–2.
9. Origen, PG. XLV, col. 1274.
10. English Translation from *Post Nicene Fathers* (1890–1892).
11. Romans 16:3–4.
12. Acts 18:1.
13. I Corinthians 16:19.
14. I Corinthians 16:11.
15. I Corinthians 16:18.
16. Acts 18:24–26.
17. Ruth Hoppin, *Priscilla Author of the Epistle to the Hebrews* (New York: Exposition Press, 1969).
18. *Codex Vaticanus 1183*, DALC. vol. 14, part 2, p. 1876.

19. A. Merk, *Novum Testamentum Graece et Latinae* (Rome: Scripta Pontifici Instituti Biblici, 60,1944), first edition 1933.
20. C. Tischendorf, *Codex Claremontanus* (Leipzig: F. A. Brochaus, 1852), p. xiv.
21. J. Gwynn, *The Book of Armagh* (Dublin: Royal Irish Academy, 1913).
22. I Corinthians 11:4.
23. Galations 3:28.
24. Colossians 3:11; Merk, *op. cit.*, p. 665.
25. Pierre Sabatier, *Bibliorum Sacrorum Latinae Versiones Antiquae seu Vetus Italica* (Paris: apud Didot, 1751), vol. 3, col. 3, 11: *"Ubi non est Masculus et Femina, Circumcisio et Praepurtim, Barbaris et Scythia, Servus et Liber."*

Appendix IV

1. Procopius of Caesara, *Secret History of the Court of the Emperor Justinian,* English translation printed by John Barkesdale (London: 1674), chaps. X and XVI.
2. Pope Leo the Great, Epistles XXX, XXXI, LXXXIV, PL. 54.
3. *Novellae* edit. G. Kroll (Berlin: Weidmannche Verlag, 1954), vol. 3, Novella. VIII, p. 90.
4. A. Debidour, *L'Impératice Théodore* (Paris: Dentu, Editeur-Libraire, 1885), p. 122.
5. Procopius, *de bello Persico,* trans. H. B. Dewing (Loeb Classical Library, 1914), p. 230.
6. Mansi, *Sacrorum Conciliorum* (Venice: 1774), vol. 13, col. 493.
7. *Ibid.,* vol. 12, p. 1153.
8. Jaffé, *Reg. Pont. Rom.* (1885), vol. 1, no. 1907, July 603, p. 213.
9. See p. 127.
10. *Theophanis Chronographia,* PG. 108, col. 932.
11. *Ibid.,* p. 932.
12. R. Holtzmann, *Geschichte der Sachischen Kaiserzeit* (München: Verlag Callweg, 1961), p. 110.
13. See p. 58.
14. Holtzmann, *op. cit.,* p. 288.
15. Turgot, *Vita Sanctae Margaretae Reginae Scotorum,* trans. W. Forbes Leith, S.J., *Life of Queen Margaret of Scotland by Turgot* (London: S.P.C.K., 1895).
16. PL. Saec. XI, col. 549.
17. Innocent IV sent a bull in 1249 confirming her canonization.
18. Clare Cross, *The Royal Supremacy in the Elizabethan Church* (London: George Allen and Unwin, 1969), p. 126.
19. John Jewel, edit. J. E. Booty, *An Apology of the Church of England* (New York: Cornell University Press, 1963), p. 31.

20. Dorothy Laird, *How the Queen Reigns* (London: Pan Books, 1961), chap. VI (first published 1959 by Hodder and Stoughton).

Appendix V

1. Marius Férotin, *Le liber Ordinum en usage dans l'Eglise Wisigothiques et mozarbc du cinquième au onzième siècle* (Paris: Librairie de Firmin-Didot, 1904), vol. 5, p. 66.
2. E. Martène, *de Antiquis Ecclesiae Ritibus* (Venice, 1736), vol. 2, p. 425.
3. Sr. Telchilde de Montessus, *Insignia Abbatium* (unpublished document in the archives of the Abbey of Notre-Dame de Jouarre, no. B.n.2., 1956).
4. Sr. Telchilde, *Vita Bertilda*, archives, Ms. 1656.
5. Sr. Telchilde, Ms. 4.
6. Antonio Francesco Frisi, *Memorie delle Chiesa Monzese* (Milan: G. Galeazzi Regio stampatore, 1774–1780), dissertazione quarta, chap. VI, p. 92: "*De rebus Sancti Johannis nullo modo se debet aliquis intromittere nisi tantum sacerdotes, qui ibi deserviunt die ac nocte, tamquam famuli et famulae, qui ibi subiecti sunt communiter debeant vivere.*"
7. H. E. Lohmann and Paul Hirsch, *Die Sachsengeschichte des Widukind von Korvei* (Hannover: Hahnsche Buchhandlung, 1935), p. 127 and note d. for the list of Mss. containing the phrase: *utriusque sexus sacerdotes* with fuller information in the introduction. The Codex of Montecassino Nr. 298^2 contains the phrase twice.
8. The Sigelberti Codex contains the variation *utriusque ordinis sacerdotes*.
9. Paul Hirsch, *Widukind Sachsische Geschichten, 955* A.D. (Leipzig: Verlag der Dyfschen Buchhandlung, funste auflage, 1931), p. 126.
10. In the Latin edition of Lohman and Hirsch as above, the line *utriusque sexus sacerdotes* occurs on p. 127.
11. Codex Steinfeld, London British Museum, Addit. 21.109, fol 175.
12. See p. 131.
13. George Fabricius, *Originum Illustrissimae Stirpis Saxonicae, libri septum* (Leipzig: Jenae, T. Steinmann, 1597). *Saxoniae Illustrati, libri novum*, is the same text as the above with two extra books added by the son of George Fabricius, Jacob Fabricius (Leipzig: 1606). Copies of these rare books can be seen at the British Museum.
14. J. Davidis Schreberi, *Vita Clarissima: Fabricius* (Leipzig: 1717). A copy of this book is available at the Staatbibliotek, Berlin, no. 10.732.

15. Bede, *Hist. Eccl.* part IV, chap. 19. Edelfrida was a deviation of the name Etheldreda. She probably only took the veil under Ebba and later became *Sacerdos Maxima* of Ely.
16. Fabricius, *op. cit.*, liber I. p. 27.
17. *Ibid.*
18. *Ibid.*, p. 44.
19. Bede, *op. cit.*, part III, chap. XXV.
20. A. W. Haddon and W. P. Stubbs, *Councils and Ecclesiastical Documents relating to Great Britain and Ireland* (Oxford: Clarendon Press, 1971), vol. 3, p. 240.
21. *Ibid.*, vol. 3, p. 264; see Chapter Five.
22. Fabricius, *op. cit.*, p. 98.
23. *Ibid.*, liber III, p. 324.
24. *Ibid.*
25. *Ibid.*, p. 331.
26. *Ibid.*, liber V, p. 542.
27. *Ibid.*, p. 555.
28. *Ibid.*, p. 586.
29. Fabricius, *op. cit.*, liber V, p. 555.
30. Walter W. Seton, *Some New Sources for the Life of Blessed Agnes of Bohemia* (Aberdeen: British Society of Franciscan Studies, 1915).
31. Reg. Vat. 18, fol 54.
32. Lucas Wadding, *Annales Minorem* (Rome: 1931), vol. 2, p. 367.
33. Fabricius, *op. cit.*, liber II, p. 100.
34. *Ibid.*, p. 104–105.
35. *Ibid.*, liber V, p. 551.
36. *Ibid.*, liber VI, p. 640.
37. F. E. Kettner, *Antiquitates Quedlinburgenses* (Leipzig: 1712), p. 152, source taken from Chron. Qued. p. 201; Tom. II, p. 117; p. 281; Tom. I. p. 351.
38. *Ibid.*, p. 169.
39. *Ibid.*, p. 274.
40. See Appendix VII.
41. Kettner, *op. cit.*, p. 289.
42. Frisi, *op. cit.*, chap. VI.
43. Schäfer, *op. cit.*, chaps. 17a and 17b, pp. 166, 167.
44. See above p. 20.
45. Daphne Pochin Mould, "Saint Brigid" *The Irish Saints* (Dublin: Clanmore and Reynolds, 1964) p. 43.
46. K. Meyer, ed. "Tertia Vita," *Anecdota Oxoniensia* (Oxford: Clarendon Press, 1885), part IV.
47. Haddon and Stubbs, *Eng. Hist Doc, Councils & Eccl. Doc.* vol. 2, part II, p. 292.
48. Meyer, *op. cit.*, p. 323.

Appendix VI

1. Mabillon, *Annales* I. p. 357 ff; Jonas, *Vita Columbanus* (1703–1739).
2. Holsten and Brockie, *Regularum Monasticarum*, Vol II.
3. *Ibid.*, p. 94.
4. Basil the Great, *Regulae Brevius*, no. 110. PG. 81, col. 1158.
5. See pp. 13–14.
6. John Neill and Helen Gamer, *An Old Irish Penitential* (New York: Columbia University Press, 1938), Records of Civilization no. 29, p. 165.
7. C. Plummer, *Vitae Sanctorum Hibernae*, vol. 1, p. 137.
8. *Ibid.*, vol. 1, chap. CXVI.
9. Martène, *de Ant. Eccl. Ritibus*, Tom. I (Antwerp: 1736), p. 746.
10. Innocent III, bull *Nova Quaedam*, 1210.
11. O. D. Watkins, *A History of Penence*, 2 vols (London: Longman, Green & Co., 1920), vol. 2.
12. *Catholic Encyclopedia* (New York: R. Appleton and Co., 1910), vol. 11, p. 624, article by Edward Hanna, "Penance."
13. See p. 65; also *Domna Sergia venerabilis diacona et abbatissa* of the monastery of *SS. Ciriaci et Nicolay* mentioned by L. M. Hartmann, *Ecclesiae Mariae in Via Lata* (Wein: Caroli Gerold, 1895), p. 19, lines 8–9; P. F. Kehr, *Regesta. Pont. Rom. Italia Pont.* (Berolini, 1906), vol. I, p. 121 which gives a letter from Sergius III to "b. Mariae Virgini et Euphemiae ven. diaconae et abbatissae"; K. H. Schäfer, Kanonissenstifter, pp. 51–60.
14. See Appendix I.

Appendix VII

1. Alberto de Capitani d'Arzago, *La Chiesa Maggiore di Milano, Santa Tecla* (Milan: Inst. di Studi Romani, Sezione Lonbarda, Casa Editrice Ceschina, 1952).
2. R. Krautheimer, "Die Doppelkathedrale in Pavia," appendix in R. Salomon, *Opicinus de Canistro* (London: Studies of the Warburg Institute, 1936).
3. *Ibid.*
4. *Ibid.*
5. C. Cecchelli, *La Baslica d'Aquileia*, cited by Krautheimer, *op. cit.*, p. 329.
6. Jean Hubert, "Les Cathédrale Double de la Gaule," in *Ganava* XI, 1963, Mélange Louis Blondel, XI, pp. 105–25; "Les Origine de Notre-Dame de Paris," in *Revue d'Histoire de l'Église de France*, L. 1964, pp. 5–24.
7. *Ibid.*
8. *Ibid.*

9. *Anonymous Ticinensis de Laudibus Papias,* ed Muratori, *Rerum Italicarum Scriptores,* XI, 19 b. (Milan: 1727).

10. C. Butler, *The Lausiac History of Palladius* (Cambridge: Texts and Studies, 1898), vol. 6, p. 212.

11. Arzago, S. Maria Maggiore was built 836 A.D.

12. G. Giulini, *Memorie Spettant alla Storia, al Governo ed alla Descrizione della Città e della Compagna di Milano* (Milan: 1760), vol. 3, p. 499.

13. *Ibid.,* vol. 1, p. 420.

14. *Ibid.,* vol. 3, p. 499.

15. S. Latuardo, *Descrizione di Milano* (Milan: 1737), vol. 1, p. 19.

16. Beroldus, *Sive Ecclesiae Amb. Med. Kalendarium et Ordinis Sae. XII,* ed. M. Magistretti (Milan: 1894), vol. 1, inf. p. 10.

17. F. Ughelli, *Italia Sacra* (Venice: apud Coleti, 1719), vol. 4, pp. 157–58.

18. See p. 12: *decumani* was the name given to clergy of Milan at the time of St. Ambrose.

19. E. Cattaneo, "*Il Clero* di S. Tecla" Appendix in the book by Arzago, *La "Chiesa Maggiore" di Milano,* p. 142; Giulini, *op. cit.,* vol. 1, p. 298.

20. Godffredo de Bussero, *Liber Notitiae Sanctorum Mediolani,* ed. Marco Magistretti and Ugo Monneret de Villard (Milan: 1913), p. 142.

21. Giulini, *op. cit.,* vol. 8, p. 259.

22. Beroldus, *op. cit.,* p. 171.

23. *Ibid.*

24. Giulini, *op. cit.,* vol. 1, p. 251.

25. George Van Wyss, *Geschichte der Abtei Zürich* (Zürich: Siebenter Bericht der antiquarischen Gesellschaft in Zürich, 1851).

Appendix VIII

1. Philibert Schmitz, *Histoire de l'Ordre de St. Benoit* (Maredsous: Fondation Universitaire de Belgique, 1956), vol. 7.

2. H. Jedin, *History of the Council of Trent,* trans. by Ernest Graf (London: Thomas Nelson, 1961), vol. 2, p. 503.

3. *Ibid.*

4. *Ibid.,* p. 521.

5. *Concilium Tridentinum,* ed. Societas Goerresiana (Freiburg: 1901), Tomus Nonus. Acta 6, p. 1076 ff.

6. J. Waterworth, *Canons and Decrees of the Council of Trent* (London: Burns and Oates, 1848), On Regulars and Nuns: chap. V, p. 240.

7. See Chapter Four.

8. See Chapter Six.

9. Archives Nationales (Paris) L.1019, no. 31.
10. See p. 155.
11. See pp. 46–47.
12. *Calendar of Close Rolls*, Edward II, 1317, p. 470.
13. Julius Normann, *Herford Chronik* (Herford: Staat-Bibliothek, 1910), p. 39.
14. See Chapter Six.
15. See Chapter Eight.
16. Waterworth, *op. cit.*, On Regulars and Nuns: chap. 9, p. 243.
17. *Ibid.*, p. 121.
18. *Concilium Tridentinum, op. cit.*, p. 1094 ff.
19. *Ibid.*, p. 1095.
20. *Ibid.*, p. 1096.
21. *Ibid.*, p. 1096.
22. Waterworth, *op. cit.*, Decree of Reformation: chap. IX, pp. 264–67.
23. See Chapter Six.
24. See Chapter Eight.
25. A. Tamburini, *de iure Abbatissarum et Monialium* (Rome: Coloniae Agrippinae, 1638).

BIBLIOGRAPHY

MANUSCRIPTS

Archives of the Abbey of Las Huelgas, Burgos: No. 30, leg 5 First papal bull giving exemption. Leg 7 No. 261, papal bull of Urban VIII. Leg 54 No. 7, writings of Jacinta de Navarra. 75. Subjection of the hospital to Las Huelgas.

Archives of Brindisi: Codice Diplomatici di Brindisi.

——: Codice Diplomatici Barese.

Archives of the Cathedral of Conversano, Italy: Pergamene 7, 16, 21, 23, and others regarding "San Benedetto" Monastery.

Archives of the Collegiate of Covarrubias, Spain: 1. No.10. A Wisigothic Ms. containing oaths of priests to an abbess.

Archives Municipales de Fontevrault, France: Registre de la Paroisse cadestre, Fol. 30v.

——: Registre des Citoyens actives. Délibérations 25v.

Archives of Notre-Dame de Jouarre: B. No. 2. *Insignia Abbatiaux* by Telchilde de Montessus.

Bibliothèque Nationale de Paris: Fr. 15697 f 197 minutes of the sessions held by Bossuet against the Abbess of Jouarre.

British Museum: *Codex Steinfeld*, Addit. 21.109, Fol. 175 re line *utriusque sexus sacerdotes* in *Rerum Gestarum Saxonicarum* by Widukind.OSB.

——: *Cotton Tiberius D. III and E.1*. Codices containing the biography of Bishop Turgot on Queen Margaret of Scotland.

——: *Cotton Faustina B. II*. Registrum de Clerkenwell. Printed in W. O. Hassall, *The Cartulary of Saint Mary of Clerkenwell*.

Mons: Bibliothèque Publique, rue des Ducs de Bourgogne. Documents officiels inédits sur l'histoire des Églises de Sainte Waudru et de Sainte Germain à Mons. Part III. p. 88 ff, No. 23.

Münster Staat Archives: VII 1007a. *Evangelia Überwasser*, containing at the back the oaths of abbesses on election, and of priests to abbesses.

Vatican Library: Reg. Vat. 17 and 18 Register of Gregory IX Reg. L3, Fol. 44–44v.

——: Vat. 9072. G. Marini, *Inscriptiones Christianes*. Part II. XXII. Inscriptions mentioning *episcopa:* a woman bishop.

PRINTED BOOKS

Anglés, H. *El Códex Musical de Las Huelgas* (1931).

Aniani, B. *Concordia Regularum*, PL. 103. Col. 950 ff.

Aquinas, Thomas. *Summa Theologica*, Vol. 3, Part III.

Arzago, A. Capitano di. *La Chiesa Maggiore di Milano: Santa Tecla.* Inst. di Studi Romani sezione Lombarda (1952).

——. *Battisteri a Milano*, cenni introduttivi alla relazione sulle scave delle Basilica di S. Tecla (1944).

Augustine St. PL. XXXIV. *Quaest in Heptateuchum.*

Auvrey, L. *Les Registres de Gregoire IX*, 2 vols. (1896–1910).

Basil the Great. *Regulae Brevius*, No. 110. PG. 81.

Bateson, Mary. *Origin and Early History of Double Monasteries,* Transactions of the Royal Historical Society. Vol. XIII (1899).

Bede, Venerable. *History of the English Church and People*, Trans. Leo Shirley-Price (1956).

Berganza, F. de *Antigüedades de España* (1719).

Beroldus. *Sive Ecclesiae Amb. Med. Kalendarium et Ordinis*, Saec. XII. Ex Codice Ambrosiano edidit M. Magistretti.

Bossuet, J. B. *Bossuet Correspondence*, ed. Urban and Levesque.

——. *Revue Bossuet* (1907).

Brindisi and Barese: Codice Diplomatici di Brindisi.

——. Codice Diplomatici di Barese.

Browe, Peter. *Beitrage zur Sexualithek des Mittelalters* (1932).

Bullettino dell'Istituto Storico Italiano (1944).

Bussero. *Liber Notitiae Sanctorum Mediolani*, ed. Magistretti (1913).

Butler, C. *The Lausiac History of Palladius*, Vol. VI (1898).

Caesarius Arelaten. *Regula Virginum*, ed. Holsten and Brockie, *Codex Regularum*, Vol. II.

Calendar Patent Rolls, 1549–51. Re Clerkenwell exemption.

Carisio, Giambatista. *De Eccles. Antiq.*

Cartulary of Saint Mary's Clerkenwell, ed. W. O. Hassall, Royal Historical Society, Vol. LXXI (1949).

Cattaneo, Enrico. *Il Clero e la Cura Pastorale nell'antico Duomo di S. Tecla* (1950). Appendix in Arzago, *La Chiesa Maggiore di milano.*

Cecchelli, C. *La Basilica d'Aquileia* (1933).

Chettle, H. F. "English Houses of the Order of Fontevrault," Reprint from *Downside Review*, Vol. LXX (1942).

Christ, Yvan. *Les Cryptes Mérovingiennes de L'abbaye de Jouarre* (1965).

Chrodegang, Bishop. *Regula Canonicarum*, PL. 89 (Ninth century).

Chrysostom, John. Homily 67. PG. 49–50.

Cogitosus, ed. Messingham. *Florilegium Insulae Sanctorum seu Vitae Acta Sanctorum Hiberniae, Vita Sanctae Brigidae.*

Colmeiro, M. *Historia General de España*, Vol. 12.

Constable, Giles. *Monastic Tithes* (1964).

Cross, Claire. *The Royal Supremacy in the Elizabethan Church* (1968).

Crowfoot, Y. *Churches of Jerash*, British School of Arch. in Jerusalem Suppl. papers (1932–33).

Danby, Herbert. *The Code of Maimonides* (1954).

Daniélou, Jean. *The Ministry of Women in the Early Church* (1961).

———. *Gregoire de Nysse* (1962).

Darp, Franz von. *Die Heberregister des Klosters Überwasser und des Stifts st. Mauritz* (1888).

Débidours, A. *L'Imperatrice Théodora* (1888).

Desguerrois, M. N. *La Sainctetè Chrétienne* (1637).

Devillers, L. *Chartres du Chapitre de Ste Waudru de Mons*, 3 vols. (1899).

Documents Officiels inédits sur l'histoire des Églises de Ste Waudru et de St. Germain à Mons, Part II.

Duplessis, Tousaint. *Histoire de l'Église de Meaux*, 2 vols (1731).

Dugdale, W. *Monasticon Anglicanum* (1655–73).

Eliensis, ed. D. J. Stewart (1848).

Escriva, Jose Maria. *La Abadessa de Las Huelgas* (1944).

Etheria. *Pilgrimage*, ed. MacClure and Feltoe.

Fabricius, G. *Originum Illustrissimae Stirpis Saxonicae* Libri VII (1597); two extra books added by Jacob Fabricius, *Saxonicae Ill* (1606).

Falco, Mario. "La Soppressione dei Conventi," *Revista d'Italia*, Anno XVII, Vol. I, No. 5 (1914).

Férotin, M. *Le Liber Ordinum en usage dans l'église Wisigothique et Mozarabe d'Éspagne du cinquième au onzième siècle*, Vol. 5 (1904).

———, *La Vierge Espagnole Etheria* (1903).

Frisi, A. F. *Memorie delle Chiesa Monzese* (1774).

Fritch, J. *Geschichte des Vormaligen Reichstifts und Stadt Quedlinburg*, 2 vols. (1838).

Funk, F. X. (ed.). *Didascalia and Const. Apost.*
Giulini, G. *Memorie di Milano,* 16 vols. (1760).
Goerres Gesellschaft. *Concilium Tridentinum* (1901 ff).
Gratien. *Decretals,* Sexte. Lib. I. Tit Vi. Cap 43.
Gregory the Great. Epistles. PL. 77–78. No. XII. Liber VII.
Gregory of Nazianzus. Epistles. No. CXCVII. English trans.: The
　　Nicene and Post Nicene Fathers. Series II. Vol. VII.
Gregory IX. Vat. Reg. 17 and 18.
Gregory of Nyssa. *Vita Sancta Macrinae Virginis,* p. 46; Trans. Low-
　　ther Clarke, *Life of St. Macrina by Gregory of Nyssa.*
Grossi-Gondi, F. *Trattato di Epigrafia Cristiana, Latine e Graece*
　　(1920).
———. *La Celebre iscrizione agriografia della basilica di S. Prassede a
　　Roma* (1916).
Guise, Jacques de. *Annals de Hainaut,* Bibliothèque Royale de Bru-
　　xelles. Reg. 9243.
Haddan, A. W. and Stubbs, W. P. *Councils and Ecclesiastical Docu-
　　ments relating to Great Britain and Ireland* (1871).
Hassall, W. O. *Cartulary of Saint Mary's Clerkenwell,* Royal Histori-
　　cal Society, Vol. LXXXXI (1949).
Herlihy, David. "Land Family and Women in Continental Europe,"
　　Traditio, Vol. XVIII (1962). Periodical, N.Y. in Studies in An-
　　cient and Medieval History.
Herzen and Rossi. *Inscriptionis Romae Latinae.*
Herzfeld, E. *Meriamlik* (1930).
———. *Monumenta Asiae Minoris Antigua,* Vol. II. Publication of
　　American Society of Archeological Research.
Hirsch, Paul. *Widukind Sächsische Geschichte* (1931).
Hirsch, S. and Lohmann, H. E. *Wittekindus Monachus Corbeiensis
　　Die Sachsengeschichte* (1935).
Holsten, Lucas. *Codex Regularum,* 2 vols. (1661).
Holtzmann, Robert. *Geschichte der Sächsischen Kaiserzeit.*
Holtzmann, Walter. *Papsturkunden in England,* Abhandlungen der
　　Wissenschaften zu Göttingen. Phil.Hist.Klasse. Neue Folge Bd.
　　25. No. 1 (1931–35, 1951).
Hoppin, Ruth. *Priscilla, Author of the Epistle to the Hebrews* (1969).
Hubert, Jean. "Les Cathedrales Doubles de la Gaule," *Genava* (Mé-
　　lange Louis Blondel) t. XI. 1963.
———. "Les Origines de Notre-Dame de Paris," *Revue d'histoire de
　　l'Église de France.* t.L. (1964).
———. *L'Art Préroman* (1936).
Huelsen, Christian. *Chiese di Roma nel Medio Evo* (1927).
Hughes, Philip. *The Reformation in England* (1963).
Ingram, J. *Saxon Chronicles,* with English Translation (1823).
Jaffé, P. Regestra Pontificum Romanorum (1885–1888), 2 vols.

James, O. E. *Marriage Customs through the Ages* (1965).

Jedin, H. *History of the Council of Trent*, 2 vols. (1959).

Jerome, Saint, PL. 25. *Epistolae*. No. XLVIII. Col. 1517.

Jewel, John. *An Apology of the Church of England*, ed. J. E. Booty (1963).

Jonas. *Vita S. Columbanus*, PL.87. Col. 1011.

Jouarre. *L'abbaye Royale Notre-Dame de Jouarre*, 2 vols. Bibliothèque d'Histoire et d'Archéologie Chrétiennes (1961).

Justinian, Emperor. *Novellae* ed. G. Kroll Vol. III (1954).

Keil J. and Wilhelm A. Keil. "Mariamlik" *Monumenta Asiae Minoris Antiqua* Publication of the American Society for Archeological Research. Vols. II and III.

Kettner, F. E. *Antiquitatis Quedlinburgensis* (1712).

———. *Kirchen und Reformations Hist. des Kaiserl. Freien Weltlichen Stifts Quedlinburg* (1710).

Kingsley-Porter, A. *Lombard Architecture*, 3 vols. (1917).

Kirsch, G. P. *The Catacombs of Rome* (1946).

Knight, M. M., I. L. Peters and Blanchard P. Peters. *Taboo and Genetics*, Part II (1921).

Knowles, D. "Essays in the Monastic History: Growth of Exemption," *Downside Abbey Review* I (1932).

Knowles, D. and Neville Hadcock. *Medieval Religious Houses in England and Wales* (1953).

Knox, John. *The First Blast of the Trumpet against the Monstrous Regiment of Women* (1557). Original printed copy in the British Museum.

Laitulliers, E. *Les Femmes de la Révolution*, 2 vols. (1900).

Lacour, L. "Rose Lacombe," *Revue Hebdomadaire* (1899).

Latuardo, S. *Descrizione di Milano*, Toms. 1–5 (1737).

LeCompt, M. *Les Privilèges de l'Abbaye de Rebais-en-Brie* (1910).

Lemarignier, Jean-François. *Étude sur les Privilèges d'Exemption et Jurisdiction Ecclésiastique des Abbayes Normandes* (1937).

Leo de Annibale. *Dell' antichissima Città di Brindisi e Oria* (1846).

Leo the Great. *Epistles* XXX, XXXI, LXXXIV. PL. 54.

Lobineau. *Histoire de Bretagne* (1707).

Lohmann, H. E. and Paul Hirsch. *Die Sachsengeschichte des Widukind von Korvei* (1935).

Loth, Bertrandus. *Resolutionibus Belgias*, Tact 9. Q.2. Art. 2.

Mabillon, J. Annales I. (1793).

———. Revue Mabillon, 1910–1914.

MacClure and Feltoe. *Palestine Pilgrims Text Society* (1897).

McKenna, M. L. *Women of the Church* (1967).

McLaughlin, T. P. *Le très ancien droit monastique de l'occident* (1935).

McNabb, Vincent O. P. "Was the Rule of St. Augustine Written for

Melania the Younger?" *Journal of Theological Studies*, No. 20. (1919).

McRoberts, David. *St. Margaret, Queen of Scotland* (1953).

Magistretti, J. *Manuale Ambrosiane*, Vols. I and II. Ed. Beroldus. See Beroldus.

Manrique, A. *Cisterciensium seu verius ecclesiasticorum annalium a condito Cistercio*, Tom. III (1642).

Mansi, D. P. *Sacrorum Conciliorum*, Nova Editio (1774) Vols. XII and XIII on Seventh General Council.

Mariana, J. *General Historia de España* (1788).

Martène. *De Antiquis Ecclesiae Ritibus*, Vols. I and II (1736, 1783).

Marucchi, O. *Basiliques et Églises de Rome* (1902).

Matthieu, Ernest. *A Travers-les-Ages* (1921).

Maxime. *L'Ésprit de la Législation Napoléonienne* (1898).

Merk, Augustine. *Novum Testamentum, Graece et Latine* (1944).

Messingham. *Florilegium Insulae Sanctorum seu vitae et Acta Sanctorum Hiberniae, Vita Sanctae Brigidae*. Cap. VI. by Cogitosus.

Mongelli, G. *Le Abbadesse Mitrate de S. Benedetto di Conversano* (1960).

Monsabert, P. de. *Le Monastère de Saint-Croix* (1952).

Montalembert, C. T. R. de, *Monks of the West* (1868).

Month, Jesuit Review, June, 1894.

Morea, D. and F. Muciaccia. *Le Pergamene di Conversano* (1942).

Mould, Daphne Pochin. *The Irish Saints* (1965).

Neill, J. and H. Gammer. *An Old Irish Penitential*, Medieval Handbooks of Penance (1938).

Nicquet, H. *Histoire de L'Ordre de Fontevrault* (1642).

Normann, J. *Herford Chronik* (1910).

Oakley, T. P. *English Penitential Discipline*, An *Anglo-Saxon Law* (1923).

Palumbo, Pier Fausto. "Il Monastero Normanno de S. Giovanni Evangelista," *Archivo Storico Pugliese* (1952).

Peers, Sir Charles and Radford C. A. Ralegh. "The Monastery of Whitby," in *Archeologia*, Vol. LXXXIX (1943).

Pernoud, R. *Aliénor d'Aquitaine* (1965).

Pidal, M. ed. Primera Canonica General de Las Huelgas.

Plummer, C. *Venerabilis Baedae*, Hist. Eccl. Vols. I and II.

Pliny the Elder. *Natural History*.

Pliny the Younger. *Epistolae*, 96 and 97.

Poignant, Simone. *L'Abbaye de Fontevrault et les Filles de Louis XV* (1966).

Potthast. *Regesta Pont. Romanorum*, Nos. 1351, 1352 (1782).

Rampolla, Cardinal. *The Life of Saint Melania the Younger* (1908).

Ridley, Jasper. *John Knox* (1968).

Rodríguez, Amancio Lopez. *El Real Monasterio Las Huelgas de Burgos y el Hospital del Rey*, 2 vols. (1907).
Rossi, G. B. *Mosaici Cristiani*, Vol. VII.
Roth, Cecil. *The Haggadah* (1934).
Schäfer, K. H. *Pharrkirche und Stift in deutschen Mittelalter* (1902).
———. *Die Kannonissenstifts in deutschen Mittelalter* (1907) (1965).
Schmitz, P. *Histoire de L'Ordre de St. Benoît*, Vol. VII (1948).
Schreberi, J. Davidis, *Vita Clarissima Viri, Georgii Fabrici* (1717).
Schulze, Rudolf. *Die Adlige Damestift und die Pfarre Liebfrauen Überwasser* (1959).
Serrano, Luciano. *Una Estigmatizada Cisterciense Doña Antonia Jacinta de Navarre y dela Cueva* (1924).
———. *Fuentes de Castilla.*
———. *Cartulario de Monisterio de Veiga* (1927).
Seton, Walter. *Some New Sources for the Life of Blessed Agnes of Bohemia* (1915).
Spellman and Wilkins, ed. *Theodore's Penitential*, Vol. III.
Steinfeld Codex. *Rerum Gestarum Saxonicorum* by Widukind.
Stengel, E. E. *Die Grabschrift der ersten Äbtissin von Quedlinburg.* Deutschen Archives für Geschichte des Mittelalter. 3. 1Abt. (1939).
Stewart, D. J. ed., *Liber Eliensis* (1848).
Tamburinius, A. *De Iure Abbatissarum et Monialium* (1638).
Telchilde de Montessus. *Insignia Abbatium*, unpublished Ms. Archives of Jouarre Bn2. (1956).
Thiercelin, H. *Les Monastères de Jouarre* (1871).
Ticinensis (Anonymous) *de Laudibus Papias*, ed. Muratori.
Tillemont, Le Nain de. *Mémoires pour servir à l'Histoire Ecclésiastique.*
Turgotus, Bishop. *Vita Sanctae Margaretae Reginae Scotorum.* Trans. W. Forbes-Leith: *Life of Queen Margaret of Scotland* (1896).
Ughelli, J. *Italia Sacra*, Tom. IV (1717).
Ure, P. N. *Justinian and His Age* (1951).
Vacca, Nicola. *Brindisi Sconosciutto* (1954).
Van Espen, D. Z. B. *Jus Ecclesiasticum Universum* (1753).
Victoria History of the Counties of England (1920).
Wadding, Lucas. *Annales Minorum*, Vols. I and II (1931).
Waterworth, J. trans. text of *The Council of Trent* (1888).
———. *Canons and Decrees of the Council of Trent* (1848).
Whitelock, Dorothy. *English Historical Documents* (1955).
Wood, M. A. E. *Lives of the Princesses of England from the Norman Conquest* (1849–55).

INDEX

Abbesses
    authority of, 2-5, 13, 21-22, 23, 45-
    52, 53-56, 59-64, 71-78, 83-88, 94,
    99
    installation of, 46, 64, 69, 71, 75,
    84, 136
    and ordination. *See* Consecrate,
    Abbesses right to
    ordination rites in sacramentaries,
    8, 13, 130
    with powers of confession, 86, 87,
    140-143
    with title of deaconess, 13, 65,
    175-176
    with title of *Sacerdos Maxima*.
    See Sacerdos Maxima
    See also proper names of abbesses
Abrissel, Robert, of Fontevrault, 46,
    47
Adelberga, Abbess, *Sacerdos Max-
    ima* of Brigg, 133
Adelheid, second wife of Otto I,
    head of Pavia, 59, 127
Adelheid of Thuringa, *Virgines
    Sacerdotes Vueisenuelsi* (with
    her sister Hedwig), 134

Adelheid II, Abbess, *Sacerdos Max-
    ima* of Quedlinburg and Gan-
    dersheim, 60
Adrian I, Pope, and Seventh Gen-
    eral Council, 125, 126
Aelfleda, Abbess, 25, 134, 143
Agde, Council of, 19
Agnes of Bohemia, *Sacerdos*, 135
Agnes I, Abbess of Notre-Dame de
    Jouarre, 37
Agnes II, Abbess of Notre-Dame de
    Jouarre, 37
Aguilberte, Abbess of Notre-Dame
    de Jouarre, 33
Alcuin of York, 63
Alexander II, Pope, 54
Alexander III, Pope, 21, 22, 23, 29,
    37, 39, 46, 54, 80, 90
Alexander IV, Pope, 27, 32, 66, 70
Alexander VIII, Pope, 44
Alexander X, Pope, 27
Alphonsus VIII, King of Castile, 83,
    84, 88, 95
Alphonsus XII, King of Castile, 95
Alphonsus XIII, King of Castile, 95
Ambrose, Saint, Archbishop of Mil-
    lan, 12, 147

Impurity of women, 2, 7, 14-15, 105-112

Innocent I, Pope, 6
Innocent II, Pope, 34, 36
Innocent III, Pope, 27, 37, 60, 61, 87, 94, 111, 142
Innocent VIII, Pope, 97
Innocent XI, Pope, 39
Inscriptions, 4-7
Irene, Empress, 16, 125-127
Irish Penitentials, 141
Irish women bishops, 14, 137, 138
Isabeau de Couhé, Abbess, 55
Isabella, Abbess, 72, 73

Jacinta of Burgos, Abbess and Mystic, 91-94
Jeanne de Lorraine, Abbess, 38
Jeanne-Baptiste de Bourbon, 51, 52, 131
Jerome, 153
Jesus
    imitation of his obedience to his mother, 45, 51-52, 101
    on contemplative life, 18
    on leadership as humble service, 101
    on marriage, 115
    women followers, 13, 113, 114, 115, 116, 117
Joanna, 114
John, Saint, evangelist, 1, 2, 6, 45, 47, 117, 157, 218
John Chrysostom, 7, 120, 121
John IV, Pope, 18, 36
John XIII, Pope, 59
John XXII, Pope, 48
Jouarre, Abbey of Notre-Dame de, 21, 27, 32-44, 50, 53, 56, 60, 61, 71, 102, 142, 152, 155, 156
Judith von Bayern, *Sacerdos*, 134
Julie-Sophie Gilette, last abbess of Fontevrault, 53
Jurisdiction
    of abbesses, 2, 7, 20, 23, 62, 72, 76, 138
    of spiritual matters by abbesses, 20, 23, 35, 40, 52, 72, 73, 76, 80, 82, 97, 98, 99
    suppressed, 82, 97, 98, 99

Justinian, Emperor, and his Code, 7, 16, 100, 125

Kettner, F. E., 58
Knox, John, 101
Kyria, Eklekta, 1, 2

Lacombe, Rose, 103
Last supper, 116, 117
Lateran Council, Fourth, 142
Laus Perennis, 14
Lecce, son of Godfrey the Norman, 80
Lecce Benedictines, 79, 80, 81
Leo, Archbishop de, 81
Leo I, Pope, 125
Leo II, Pope, 70
Leo IV, Emperor, 125
Leonora, Queen of Castile, 83, 84, 87, 88
Lérin, Abbot of, 19
Leviticus, 107-108
Loth, Bertrand, 103
Louis XIII, King of France, 51
Louise de Bourbon, Abbess, 131
Lucius III, Pope, 28, 59
Lutheran faith, 39, 61
Lydia, follower of Saint Paul, 119

Macrina, founder of Basilian Order, 13, 14
Madame Maintenon, 53
Maimonides Code Book, 108
Malcolm, King of Scotland, 127, 128
Marcellina, 147
Margaret, Queen of Scotland, 42, 84, 127-129
Margueritea de Rohan, Abbess, 60
Marie de Bretagne, Abbess, 49, 50, 55, 102, 151
Marie de Tremoille, Abbess, 38
Marie Madeleine Gabrielle de Rochechouart, 52, 53, 152
Marthana, deaconess, 13
Martin I, Pope, 36
Martin V, Pope, 65
Mary and Martha, 115
Mary, mother of Jesus, 5, 13, 45, 57, 114, 115, 117, 158
Mary, mother of James, 114